OVERCOMING
OUR
COMPULSIONS

OVERCOMING OUR COMPULSIONS

USING THE
TWELVE STEPS
AND THE
ENNEAGRAM
AS SPIRITUAL
TOOLS FOR LIFE

Mary E. Mortz

Triumph™ Books
Liguori, Missouri

Published by Triumph™ Books
Liguori, Missouri 63057-9999
An Imprint of Liguori Publications

Scriptural citations are taken from the *New Revised Standard Version*. Copyright © 1989 by the division of Christian Education of the National Council of Churches in the United States of America. Used with permission.

The Twelve Steps (see page 179) are reprinted and adapted with the permission of Alcoholics Anonymous World Services, Inc. Permission to reprint and adapt the Twelve Steps does not mean that AA has reviewed or approved the content of this publication, nor that AA agrees with the views expressed herein. AA is a program of recovery from alcoholism. Use of the Twelve Steps in connection with programs and activities which are patterned after AA but which address other problems does not imply otherwise.

Library of Congress Cataloging-in-Publication Data

Mortz, Mary.
      Overcoming our compulsions: using the twelve steps and the enneagram as spiritual tools for life/Mary Mortz.
      p.   cm.
      Includes bibliographical references (p. 173-174) and index.
      ISBN: 0-89243-688-3
      1. Spiritual life. 2. Twelve-step programs—Religious aspects.
3. Enneagram.   I. Title.
BL624.M667 1994
291.4'4—dc20
                                             94-7494
                                               CIP

Thank You

To you, my God,
To you, my teachers:
    David, Eileen, Helen, Julia, Ken, Kacey,
    Margaret, Marge, Mary, Muriel, Ned, Pat,
    Pauline, Susie, and Melodie

To those of you who have blessed me
    by allowing me to share
    your journey with you

To those of you who have encouraged me
    so much on my own journey and
    helped me through the preparation of
    this book…

    my Religious Sisters:
        the Daughters of Mary and Joseph,
    my parents and my brothers and sisters,
    my many wonderful friends

Contents

Figures   **X**

Acknowledgments   **XI**

Preface   **XIII**

Part 1: **Learning About the Twelve Steps and the Enneagram**   **1**

Chapter 1: The Twelve Steps in Action 3
Chapter 2: So, What Is This Enneagram? 9
    Where Is Your Center? 12

Part 2: **Steps One, Two, Three and the Enneagram Points** **19**

Chapter 3: Step One: Awk! I'm Stuck!!! 21
    Through the Eyes of the Enneagram 23
        About the One 25
        About the Two 30
        About the Three 35
        About the Four 40
        About the Five 46
        About the Six 52
        About the Seven 57
        About the Eight 63
        About the Nine 68
Chapter 4: Step Two: Begin to Really Believe .. 79
Chapter 5: Step Three: Turn It Over 83

Part 3: **Steps Four Through Eleven**   **89**

Chapter 6: Step Four: Take a Good Look at Yourself 91
Chapter 7: Step Five: Share Step Four with Someone 103
Chapter 8: Step Six: Getting Ready to Let Go! 105

Higher Point One 106
Higher Point Two 107
Higher Point Three.......................... 108
Higher Point Four 108
Higher Point Five 109
Higher Point Six 110
Higher Point Seven........................... 111
Higher Point Eight 112
Higher Point Nine 113
Chapter 9: Step Seven: Let Go! 117
Chapter 10: Step Eight: Look Again at Your
Behavior 119
Chapter 11: Step Nine: Find Ways to Make
Amends 125
Chapter 12: Step Ten: Ongoing Maintenance Is a
Must 129
Chapter 13: Step Eleven: Keeping Contact with
Your Source 141

Part 4:   Continuing With the Enneagram   153
Chapter 14: Step Twelve: Carry the Message to
Others 155

Part 5:   Concluding Thoughts   161
On Two Steppers 163
On Five Steppers 164
On Humility, Not Humiliation 165
On Your Special Companion 166
On the K.I.S.S. Method 168
On Learning More 169

Part 6:   Appendices   171
Appendix 1: Resources 173
Appendix 2: AA Sources and the Twelve Steps 175
The Twelve Steps As Written by
Alcoholics Anonymous 179
Appendix 3: Scriptures Used in Appendices ... 181
Appendix 4: Scriptures and Twelve Steps 183
Step One: Surrender 183

Step Two: Belief 189
Step Three: Decision, Commitment .. 194
Step Four: Examination, Inventory 196
Step Five: Admit Your Defects 200
Step Six: Become Ready to Ask 201
Step Seven: Ask for Release 201
Step Eight: Make Amends List 203
Step Nine: List of Amends 204
Step Ten: Maintain Growth 205
Step Eleven: Conscious Contact 207
Step Twelve: Share 211
Appendix 5: Scriptures and Enneagram Points 217
Point One 217
Point Two 220
Point Three 227
Point Four 233
Point Five 237
Point Six 242
Point Seven 250
Point Eight 254
Point Nine 262

Index   269

About the Author   273

Figures

Figure 1: The Three Levels of the Twelve Steps 6
Figure 2: The Enneagram 10
Figure 3: Some Enneagram Titles 14
Figure 4: The Enneagram Stress Points 15
Figure 5: The Enneagram Security Points 16
Figure 6: Point One 25
Figure 7: Point Two... 30
Figure 8: Point Three 35
Figure 9: Point Four 40
Figure 10: Point Five 46
Figure 11: Point Six 52
Figure 12: Point Seven 57
Figure 13: Point Eight.. 63
Figure 14: Point Nine 69
Figure 15: Inventory List: Times I Have Been Angry
            or Resentful.. 94
Figure 16: Instincts/Subtypes Affected (Column Three) 95
Figure 17: Times I Have Been Afraid 97
Figure 18: Sample Writing on Fear 98
Figure 19: Times I Have Been Harmed or Done Harm to Others 99
Figure 20: Sample Writing on Harms and Hurts 100
Figure 21: Enneagram Points: Higher Traits,
            Virtues, Fruits, Gifts, Blessings 114
Figure 22: Sample Amends List 121
Figure 23: Revised Amends List 122
Figure 24: Mini-Inventory List.. 131
Figure 25: The Enneagram Lower Traits 134
Figure 26: The Enneagram Instincts/Subtypes 135
Figure 27: The Enneagram and the Stress Points 136
Figure 28: The Enneagram and the Security Points 136
Figure 29: Reflection Headstone: Who I Was 148
Figure 30: Reflection Headstone: Who I Am........................... 149
Figure 31: Reflection Headstone: Whom I Am
            Invited to Become 149

Acknowledgments

The content of this book is a result of thirty years of "walking with others" in search of spiritual growth. These individuals include friends from a wide variety of circumstances. Some individuals are deeply invested in a particular church or religion. Others have no specific church affiliation but have strong ties to recovery programs dealing with various addictive patterns or diseases. Still others have neither churches nor recovery programs but, like the rest, share the same hunger for a fuller, more compassionate, loving, and just life through a relationship with a God.

I have learned much from each of these people, my friends. They have shown me the tools that have been helpful in their growth. Through them I have been able to utilize those same tools and others I have discovered through research in my own spiritual journey. These people, and this journey, have brought me to the gifts of the Enneagram and the Twelve Steps, which I have used almost exclusively. Since I found these two systems, I have been able to incorporate them into retreats and workshops with great success for all involved.

Over time, an increasing number of people began asking me for more information, encouraging me to write a book detailing the use of the combined systems for personal spiritual development. This book is my response to their loving encouragement. It has been a pleasure to share in the very real transformations of many people who were already so good! They have developed a sensitivity to themselves, to society, and to our planet.

I pray that the tools of this book find their way into the hands of those they can help. Please accept the book with my love.

Preface

Is this book for you? It is written with three groups of people in mind.

The first group consists of those of you who are in Twelve Step programs such as Alcoholics Anonymous[1], Al-Anon, Codependents Anonymous, Emotional Health Anonymous, Overeaters Anonymous, and so forth. You are already living this simple program of rigorous honesty, self-reflection, making amends, and reevaluation. You already know that by "working your program," you are open to growing more and more each day, but you seek to observe yourself more accurately and to learn what "grabs your attention." You have come to know that what you give your attention to is what directs your life. You wish to understand further how you can more deeply relate to others and your God. If you are in this group, the Enneagram can assist you.

The second group also has as its members those of you who already know and use the Enneagram. You have studied this system and know it has helped you to understand how you pay attention, how you respond to what you experience as stress, and how you respond when you feel secure or when growth is happening. You know this "Map of Nine" is the result of developed study of the nine personality types by Gurdjieff and Ichazo[2] and is consistent with many ancient approaches to growth, including Jewish and Early Christian traditions of understanding behavior. You can recognize the traditions of the Enneagram's seven basic fixations, or compulsions, plus two other traits/defects: self-deceit and paralyzing fear. You are aware that these fixations and traits are intended as a guide for individuals who wish to improve the understanding each has for self and others.

Taken alone, each approach is dynamic and effective. However, when they are combined, a double effect seems to take place. The language and system of the Enneagram has helped those already in

Twelve Step programs to understand individual compulsions and gifts more clearly. The simple, clear method of the Twelve Steps has helped many a good "self-observer" to extend and deepen his or her own chosen path.

The third group I wish to address consists of those of you who are familiar with neither the Twelve Steps nor the Enneagram, but who wish to find tools with which you can further develop your growing spirituality. Through these pages, I hope to supply you with the materials I have found to be greatly beneficial in promoting emotional and spiritual growth to those from all walks of life.

There is a fourth group for whom I did not write this book specifically. It may be that you have been "led" to pick it up. It is now in your hands. Please read it with care. Read not only with your head, but with your heart as well. You are welcome to practice the journey described in this book. If you do not find these supplies helpful, there are many other resources, methods, and systems available for you to draw upon.

In the ensuing pages you will find easy-to-understand explanations of both the Twelve Step and the Enneagram systems. They were written so you can refer to them as needed for further understanding as you begin to grasp and utilize the information you find in the remainder of the book.

Notes

[1] The letters "AA" will be used to refer to Alcoholics Anonymous from this point on.

[2] The role of Gurdjieff and Ichazo is reported in the works of Goldberg, O'Leary, Palmer, and Rohr. These references are included in Appendix 1 in Part 6.

PART 1

*Learning
About the
Twelve Steps
and the
Enneagram*

Chapter 1

The Twelve Steps in Action

The Twelve Steps are a series of tools used by people who partici-pate in programs such as Alcoholics Anonymous (AA). They were developed by a group of alcoholics who found that, in order to over-come their specific disease, they needed to follow a very simple, clear, honest lifestyle that centered on the presence of a Higher Power in their lives. Over time, this method, when followed and practiced dili-gently, has proved to help change and improve the lives of thousands of individuals who previously suffered from various life-threatening addictive/compulsive diseases.

Perhaps those who wrote the first Twelve Steps in AA realized that as they faced their disease and their character defects they became stronger. Their lives became good, not only for themselves but for the others around them. They soon found that the Twelve Steps were, in fact, a spiritual journey, and that all the areas of their lives became permeated by the principles of the spiritual journey.

In this spiritual journey when we use the Twelve Steps, we see that the Steps are being applied repeatedly in all areas of life. New insights are constantly being revealed as challenges to grow in at least one of these areas, if not more, at any given time. The Twelve Steps present, in a systematic way, a method for growth that has proved to help change the lives of thousands of persons.

Perhaps it is no coincidence that in the Old Testament the Chosen People were in twelve tribes. In the New Testament, Jesus selected twelve apostles, and now among us we find a new resource in the spiritual program laid out in the Twelve Steps! Sometimes it seems strange that a program such as the Twelve Steps of AA can have such an influence on so many lives. The pace with which the influence of the Twelve Steps is spreading can seem surprising. It can appear to be a fad or an accidental trend. I would offer the following thought if this is your view.

In the Twelve Step programs' "folklore" there is a definition of the word *accident* or *coincidence*. An accident or a coincidence is defined as "a miracle when God chooses to remain anonymous."

What follows is a paraphrased version of the Twelve Steps so you can see how anyone can apply these simple principles in daily life. Each Step is followed by a brief explanation of what it entails.

Step One: Powerless, Unmanageable. "Awk, I'm Stuck." I admit that I am powerless over life, over others, and over myself. My life has become, in some way, unmanageable.

Step Two: Come to Believe. "God Can." I come to believe that there is a power greater than just myself in this world, here and now. I am not "it." I don't have to pretend that I am the Higher Power for myself or for others. This Higher Power can restore me to a happy, fruitful, whole, and sanely balanced life.

Step Three: Decide to Turn It Over. "Let Him." I accept to make the decision to surrender, to "let go and let God" take over in my life. I agree to allow God to care for me, and to cooperate with him.

Step Four: My Personal Inventory. When I am ready and without fear, I accept the challenge to look at my entire life. I review (re-view) my patterns of feeling, my relationships, my work, my play, and my sex life. I look at the harms and hurts I have experienced, as well as those that I have done to others.

Step Five: Admit It. I share my Fourth Step insights with another person. I "confess" them, admitting everything to someone I trust.

Step Six: Become Ready to "Let Go." I review Steps One through Five again. I look at my character gifts and defects that have surfaced. I pray for the willingness to let God remove the defects and to fill the void that I so fear. I pray for the willingness to use my gifts as he sees fit.

Step Seven: Ask God to Remove My Character Defects. I ask God to take away any negative patterns of feeling, responding, thinking, I have that are stumbling blocks for me or for others.

Step Eight: Make My "Amends List." I prepare a list of anyone and any institutions I have harmed or hurt in any way.

Step Nine: Make the Amends. I go about the task of expressing sorrow where necessary, and I work to make right the wrongs I have done, if this is possible.

Step Ten: Continue to Take My Personal Inventory. I continue to examine my "conscience" for the good and the not so good of my life. I do this on a daily basis.

Some refer to this as taking Steps One through Nine every day. (With practice, this becomes simpler.) Others refer to Step Ten as taking Steps Two through Nine. The distinction is not vital. What is necessary is to do it!

Step Eleven: Maintain a Conscious Contact With God. I let God in every day. I allow space and open the door to an awareness of my Higher Power in my life. I remain open to learning to listen to God, to communicate with him. I allow his love to deepen in me and to flow out into all the areas of my life.

Step Twelve: Carry This Message to Others. Having experienced new life and growth, I share my newly found life with others. I find respectful, nonintrusive ways to do this. I practice my newly found "life habits," my new principles, in all the aspects of my life.

The basic work of these Twelve Steps can be divided into three levels of activity. Figure 1 presents these three levels in a visual form.

FIGURE 1A

THE THREE LEVELS OF THE TWELVE STEPS

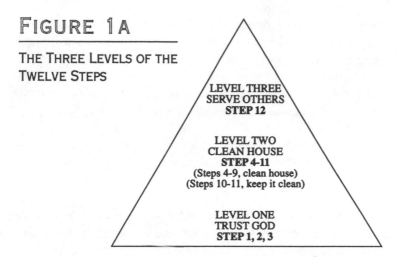

LEVEL THREE
SERVE OTHERS
STEP 12

LEVEL TWO
CLEAN HOUSE
STEP 4-11
(Steps 4-9, clean house)
(Steps 10-11, keep it clean)

LEVEL ONE
TRUST GOD
STEP 1, 2, 3

FIGURE 1B

THE THREE LEVELS OF THE TWELVE STEPS

Level	Activity	Twelve Steps
One	Trust God	1,2,3
Two	Clean House	4-9: Clean inner house 10-12: Keep it clean
Three	Serve others	12

Level One can be summarized as "Trust God." This includes Steps One through Three. It is here that you come to a profound sense of what it means to have something greater than yourself and your ego in life. You learn to give this something a name,[1] even if the name is "Higher Power." For the purposes of this book, this "Higher Power" will be called "God." Eventually, in Step Three, you become ready to trust this God with your life. You then decide to make the commitment to do so.

Level Two can be summarized as "Clean House." This consists of Steps Four through Eleven. The task is to do what it takes to clean your inner house (Steps Four through Nine) and to continue to keep it clean (Steps Ten through Eleven). You learn to observe your feelings when they occur, to view your actions objectively, and to make up for your wrong or harmful actions.

You learn to remain focused by learning how to maintain a daily, conscious contact with God. Those who live by the principles inherent in these Steps report that they see and experience life clearly as never before, "as if with a new pair of glasses."[2]

Level Three can be summarized as "Serve Others." This is articulated in Step Twelve. This new way of seeing and experiencing your inner and outer worlds flows naturally into service to others. In Step Twelve you come to the realization that your new life principles are automatically overflowing into every aspect of your life. As a result of your spiritual awakening, you experience a hunger, an inner longing, a desire to practice these principles in all your affairs.

This new spiritual way of life overflows into your sexual and intimate relationships, into your relationships at work, and into the many activities in which you engage. Your new attitude affects your community-outreach activities, your volunteer service projects, and your recreational pursuits.

When you become free of the personal compulsions and addictions that hold you in bondage, a new energy emerges. Your world becomes much bigger. You develop a new sensitivity. You see whole new ways to serve others. You realize that there are gifts and strengths within you that have never been available before. You find yourself happily involved with your own little corner of life with a heart full of love and compassion for others. Surprisingly, from your love and energy, a ripple effect spreads out to others to extend the love beyond you.

It is this overflowing ripple effect that has led the Twelve Steps to touch the lives of so many people. In AA, members speak of the Twelve Step program as a "program of attraction, not promotion." Others want what we have. As each one practices the Twelve Steps, others see the effects, and they are touched.

A word of caution might be offered here. It can be a temptation to approach the Twelve Steps rationally through your mind. It can be a temptation to spend time analyzing why these Steps work. Though this is an interesting exercise, it can be an avoidance of doing the actual work of these Twelve Steps. The invitation is to dig in, to use your heart sensitively. Let your gut-level instincts work with your thinking mind.

An analogy might be that you can read volumes of inspirational articles about exercise. You can study the science of how to begin a walking program "until the cows come home." If, however, you do not get out there and put one foot in front of the other, you are not going to go very far. Being in good shape does not come by osmosis.

Chapter 2

So, What Is This Enneagram?

The Enneagram (pronounced "ee-nee-uh-gram"), as stated in the Preface, means a map or measure of nine and is a system rooted in principles consistent with those of Jewish and early Christian traditions. It was brought to the United States in the early 1970s by Oscar Ichazo. Gurdjieff[3] worked with the teachings and formulated the basic circle chart with the nine points at their present locations. Religious orders, especially the Jesuits, received it and made use of it for spiritual development, keeping the method a secret as they were instructed to do. If they instructed others in it, they required the students to keep the instruction secret. Other dedicated individuals, including Naranjo, Palmer, Rohr, Beesing, and O'Leary, have made significant contributions to this system's further research, growth, and utilization as a spiritual training method.

Naranjo studied the system with Ichazo in Chile, then brought it back to Esalen, where he developed it further as ways in which we protect ourselves, our "egos." Helen Palmer, one of his students, continued the investigation of the Enneagram and presented an excellent work on the Enneagram in 1988. This is intended as a guide to those of us wishing to better understand ourselves and others.

In the 1980s a steady supply of books and tapes became available, beginning with the work of Beesing, Nogosek, and O'Leary.[4]

The Enneagram is a system of nine Personality Points represented in a circular figure. (See Figure 2.) Each Point or "type" is located in one of three centers: the "feeling" center, the "mind" center, or the "gut" center. Each center has a core or midpoint. The Point to either side of the core is called the "Wing" of the Point.

Through the Enneagram system, you learn to pay attention to the things that "grab" your attention. You learn to observe yourself honestly by looking deeply at yourself and your behaviors. This way you are able to determine which Personality Point on the Enneagram best describes you, using the descriptive information provided. Through this system you find information to help you face your chief preoccupation, determine your protective buffers, and understand the protective mechanisms you have used throughout your life.

FIGURE 2

THE ENNEAGRAM

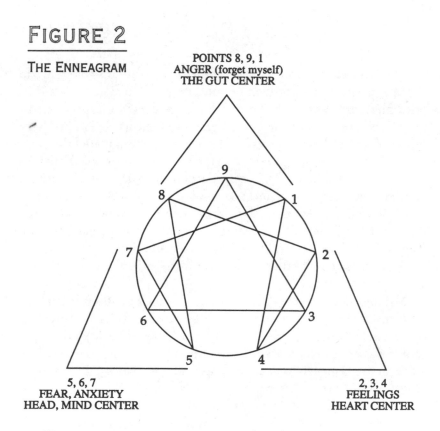

POINTS 8, 9, 1
ANGER (forget myself)
THE GUT CENTER

5, 6, 7
FEAR, ANXIETY
HEAD, MIND CENTER

2, 3, 4
FEELINGS
HEART CENTER

The Enneagram is not all about negatives, however. This self-evaluation allows you to look at the negatives in your life and personality and, if you choose, to turn them into positives by making them the basis for change in your life. These are the invitations to transformation that wait for you. These are the invitations to transformation that will lead you to your personality type's true gifts and blessings. Part of that journey you undertake in the process helps you walk through your old habits, your dark negatives, so you can really value the true light of all of your gifts and strengths that, for whatever reason, are not as available to you in your life.

The remainder of this section briefly summarizes the Personality Points briefly. Much of the discussion is gleaned from information that others have shared with me from their lives, as well as from the professional training sessions by Palmer and Daniels, workshops by O'Leary, the writings of Palmer, Rohr, Beesing, Nogosek, and O'Leary, Dobson, and Hurley and Riso.

Where Is Your Center?

In the feeling or heart center the feelings are used as a primary frame of reference. Reality is filtered through an intuition based upon feelings. This does not mean that those in the other two centers do not have feelings, but that in this center feelings are a primary source for perceiving reality and responding to it. Persons in this center do not know how they are feeling so much as they use feelings to get cues for responding to others.

The types in this center are the Twos, the Threes, and the Fours.

The Two has been called the "Giver" (Palmer); the "Need to Be Needed" (Rohr); the "Helper" (Riso); "Egocentric Generosity" (Naranjo); the "Assistant" (Beesing, Nogosek, and O'Leary).

If you are a Two, you change yourself and your feelings to accommodate others; you shift your attention to focus on the needs of others.

The Three has been called the "Performer" (Palmer); the "Need to Succeed" (Rohr); the "Status Seeker" (Riso); "Success Through Appearance" (Naranjo); the "Administrator" (Beesing, Nogosek, and O'Leary). The Three is the center point of this feeling or heart center.

If you are a Three, you are not necessarily in touch with your own feelings or with your relationship with others. You use feelings to sense what is necessary. You see everything as "networking" toward a goal. Your identity is based in your project(s).

The Four has been called the "Tragic-Romantic" (Palmer); the "Need to be Special" (Rohr); the "Artist" (Riso); "Seeking Happiness Through Pain" (Naranjo); the "Author" (Beesing, Nogosek, and O'Leary).

If you are a Four, you take your feelings inward and hold on to them. You view yourself as special, unique, and sensitive but can actually be very insensitive to others because you remain focused on yourself instead of reaching out to assist or nurture others in need.

In the mind or head center the mode of perceiving is through a filtering of reality by the thinking mind. The major motivation is to have protection from fear. The types in this center are the Fives, the Sixes, and the Sevens.

The Five has been called the "Observer" (Palmer); the "Need to Perceive" (Rohr); the "Thinker" (Riso); and "Seeking Wholeness

Through Isolation" (Naranjo); the "Sage" (Beesing, Nogosek, and O'Leary).

If you are a Five, you respond to fear by backing away from the outside threat. You can be very active and busy externally, but you have removed your basic self into a "balcony seat" in life.

The core of this head center is the Six. The Six has been called the "Devil's Advocate" (Palmer); the "Need for Security/Certainty" (Rohr); the "Loyalist" (Riso); the "Persecuted Persecutor" (Naranjo); the "Facilitator" (Beesing, Nogosek, and O'Leary).

If you are a Six, you observe the outer world for potential harm. You either withdraw from harm or go against it to gain the illusion of being safe from it.

The Seven has been called the "Planner or Epicure" (Palmer); the "Need to Avoid Pain" (Rohr); the "Generalist" (Riso); "Opportunistic Idealism" (Naranjo); the "Optimist" (Beesing, Nogosek, and O'Leary).

If you are a Seven, you respond to fear by being almost oblivious to it. You direct your focus in life to planning many things at the same time. Your mind pays attention to ideas and ways to receive stimulation from many activities and ideas. You look to the fun in life, avoiding the recognition of pain.

Those in the body or gut center are the Eights, the Nines, and the Ones.

The Eight has been called the "Boss" (Palmer); the "Need to be Against" (Rohr); the "Leader" (Riso); "Coming on Strong" (Naranjo); the "Champion" (Beesing, Nogosek, and O'Leary).

If you determine that you are an Eight, you are aware that you fill yourself with experiences and personal indulgence. You are comfortable expressing anger, although you don't know why you feel it. Your issue as an Eight is to have control over your space and personal boundaries. It is important for you to protect the people and things you perceive are within the boundary of your terrain. This makes almost everything your responsibility.

The core Point in this body or gut center is the Nine, the "Mediator" (Palmer); the "Need to Avoid" (Rohr); the "Peacemaker" (Riso); "Going with the Stream" (Naranjo); the "Negotiator" (Beesing, Nogosek, and O'Leary).

If you are a Nine, you can feel and express anger safely if it is for a "just" cause and not related directly on your own behalf. You do not routinely express your own wishes and needs. It seems as if you are asleep to their existence and you yourself exist by merging with the energy and views going on around you. You are able to see and understand opposing opinions equally well.

The One is called the "Perfectionist" (Palmer); the "Need to be Perfect" (Rohr); the "Reformer" (Riso); "Angry Virtue" (Naranjo); the "Inspector" (Beesing, Nogosek, and O'Leary).

If you are a One, you have a lid tightly sealed on your anger. You are usually the last to know that you even have angry feelings. You avoid anger. For you to show anger is completely unacceptable. However, to feel resentment toward others for their actions and to correct them is acceptable if they are not doing the right thing (as you see it). As a One, goodness and rightness are derived from within yourself and your perceptions of the world.

Figure 3 presents a summary of the titles of the Enneagram Points referred to in this book.

FIGURE 3

SOME ENNEAGRAM TITLES

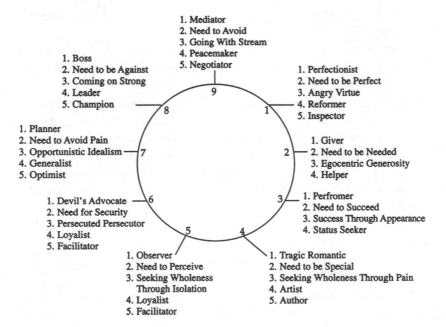

In addition to the terminology you will use to recognize your compulsions and defects, the Enneagram gives precious assistance to help you view how you operate when you are truly under stress. The "trigger" issue or reason is distinct for each Point. When overload occurs, you can respond by taking on traits seen at another Point on the Enneagram. The movement is predictable. If you look at Figure 4, you will note that the Enneagram is diagrammed with arrows in it.

FIGURE 4[7]

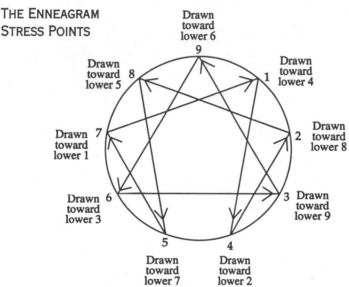

THE ENNEAGRAM
STRESS POINTS

Drawn toward lower 6
9

Drawn toward 8 lower 5

Drawn toward 1 lower 4

Drawn toward 7 lower 1

Drawn toward 2 lower 8

Drawn 6 toward lower 3

3 Drawn toward lower 9

5

4

Drawn toward lower 7

Drawn toward lower 2

When pushed beyond your limits, when overstressed, you move in the direction of the arrow, "going with the flow." You draw upon the lower characteristics of your "stress" point. This movement is referred to as your Stress Point. The movement is unique for each Point.

This can be of great value as you learn to observe yourself and how you operate under stress. When you use the Twelve Steps along with the self-observation of the Enneagram, you get the skills to change your pattern of "sliding" or "coasting," once you have gained the insight of its power in your life.

The Enneagram also presents valuable insights as to how you operate when you are becoming transformed and are behaving in a generous, life-giving way. As a person, you develop the higher gifts and traits of your own Point and take on the higher aspects of your Security Point. Figure 5 indicates the direction you would follow in this part of your journey, your growth. You might view the work involved for this movement to happen as being similar to nature's design, where the salmon must swim upstream to come home to plant their eggs to let new life happen.

FIGURE 5[8]

THE ENNEAGRAM SECURITY POINTS

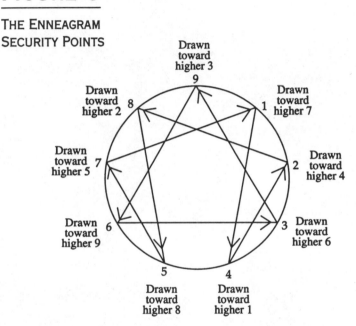

A word of caution is suggested. The challenge is for you to observe your own "self," your Point, and how you operate. Your growth is truly your own. Sometimes you might find that you call upon the gifts, the higher aspects, located within your Stress Point. Instead of observing only the lower aspects of your Stress Point, it is also helpful to observe the lower aspects located within your Security Point.

As you experience yourself hungry for "more" in your life, as you grow and develop, you become what is called a "seeker." You continue to live, observing yourself, your patterns, your responses. You become ready to do the work of walking a spiritual path, the journey of transformation.

Your task as a spiritual seeker is to remain honest, open, and willing to look at yourself regardless of whatever movement is happening. Life is inviting you to listen to your own experience, to learn to observe the way you "place your attention." You are invited on a profound and beautiful journey of complete personal integration and transformation.

Notes

[1]Many eventually call their Higher Power, God, or a more specific title. This happens gradually as they grow in a specific relationship with their understanding of God. Some, however, hold their conception of God as the love in the group, or nameless being within.

[2]"C," Chuck. *A New Pair of Glasses* (Irvine: New Look Publishing Co., 1984).

[3]Authors who discuss the development of the Enneagram in the United States are Beesing, Nogosek, and O'Leary; Goldberg, Palmer, Riso, and Rohr. These are listed in Appendix 1 in Part 6.

[4]Maria Beesing, Robert J. Nogosek, and Patrick O'Leary, *The Enneagram* (Denville, NJ: Dimension Books, 1984).

[5]When you experience resistance, discomfort, "stress," each Point becomes more open to experience the weaker, more negative traits of its own Point, and of its Stress Point. You do this as a way to cope and function in a way you feel will be safe for you.

[6]When comfortable, when growing, "when feeling secure," each Point becomes more open to experience the strengths of its own Point as well as the higher aspects of its Security Point. When this happens, it is as if you are hungering for more in yourself as you grow and develop.

PART 2

Steps One, Two, Three and the Enneagram Points

Chapter 3

Step One: Awk! I'm Stuck!!!

Step One: We admitted we were powerless over life and life's conditions, and that our lives had become unmanageable.[1]

Some people who have already looked at the list of the Twelve Steps may find some other step to be more difficult or more threatening to them. For most people, though, the most difficult Step, the most disgusting, is this Step One. It goes against your natural instincts to admit that you do not have control.

Ironically, it is the content of Step One that is also the content of the first be-attitude (beatitude).[2] This is the actual basis for the spiritual journey, yet most individuals have the greatest difficulty with this concept. You always find yourself "taking back" and returning to your basic flaw. What mature adult in today's world wants to perceive himself or herself as powerless!

The journey begins when you finally are ready to look hard at your own deception. You have to get to this point to be ready for Step One, or the other Steps have no real meaning. They can be an interesting exercise for self-improvement, but a real, spiritual revolution[3], the real 180-degree change of life, does not happen unless you take Step One.

The task of letting go of the darkness in your life does not happen simply by willing it in your head, in your heart, or in your gut. You have to admit how much the defect or habit or trait is part of you; how much it operates you, before Step One can happen. When this awareness dawns, your journey begins. When you see where you have focused your attention, you are ready to take a big "gasp of surprise," to surrender, to "let go," to get going on the conversion path.

To walk this path is humbling and rugged. This is against human instinct. Without knowing it, it is natural to exist while resisting surrender. To give up and to admit your real powerlessness over others, and even over yourself, is something you resist at a very deep core level. Each of us has been conditioned by life at some level to act as if we are in control. We have learned to hide our true feelings, to function well.

The first of the Twelve Steps invites you to admit you have a problem. In some deep and personal way, you know you are not yet the person you need to become. You do not even know who that person is. You need help on this path. When you can realize your own need, your own personal "poorness," your poverty, you are actually taking Step One. You are becoming ready to let God in so he can have a real place in your life.

The "life condition" that causes trouble may be different for each individual. It may be a personality compulsion that has worked for you so far, but it just isn't working any longer. Your "life condition" may be other people who trouble you and with whom you become frustrated or hurt. It may be that you avoid allowing yourself to face your own needs.

There are many ways to avoid facing your fragility. Perhaps you're too busy, hiding from relationships by engaging in too many activities, projects, work, books, too much "people pleasing." You can hide in what is viewed as your own special feeling or pain. You can think you are being spiritual, but in reality you may be blocking out others, protecting yourself from being seen as you really are.

Sometimes you hide your powerlessness in thinking you are unique—so special that no one could ever really understand you or how you feel. Perhaps you hide your tender little marshmallow inside by presenting a gruff or hostile front. You might hold people at a distance in case they try to relate to you tenderly, thus exposing your vulnerability. You might "melt" and get hurt.

Sometimes your fear shows through deviance in your behavior. You may speak so as to dominate others or to "show off." Deviance may be seen in a misuse of alcohol, legal or illegal drugs, food, sex, or in antisocial activities. All these patterns can be ways to avoid facing your anger, fear, or anxiety.

Some of you hide in withdrawal behaviors. Withdrawal can be a passive pattern when you are faced with conflict or abuse. It can be a habitual response of standing back and observing life, studying it, reading about it, and living only vicariously through the experiences of others.

If you really want to take Step One honestly, share your reflections with at least one other person. When you reflect openly with another human being, your awareness grows, and you begin to see the wonderful possibilities of Step One.

As you observe yourself openly, you become aware that, in some way, deep within yourself, you *do* have a need for God. In some way your life is not really manageable by yourself. You recognize that you do, indeed, need a new habit, a new way of responding, a happier, more honest, more relational, more secure life inside your own skin or with others or maybe with your God.

Through the Eyes of the Enneagram

Using the Enneagram in Step One gives you a tool to see clearly *the thing* you need to change. Each person is usually the last one to see the "log in his or her own eye" or to do something about it.[4] The Enneagram helps you see what you pay attention to, so that no room for doubt remains as to the path you can walk if you accept help to see your area(s) of insanity, your imbalance, and your powerlessness.

There are volumes written on the Enneagram. The approach of this work is to present principal traits that can help you "find your Point." References with more extensive discussion are offered in Appendix 1 in Part 6. I would encourage their use. There is much, much more to this system than can be presented in this summary.

In this chapter, only the basic characteristics of each Point will be presented. If you recognize some of your own personal traits, remain open to the possibility for growth. Stay open to the insights that will show how much the compulsion of this Point does in fact hold you out of balance, not whole, not sane. Stay open to admitting the extent to which you are your traits. Stay open to observing the extent to which your life is not manageable.

One way to identify the patterns you use to operate is to put a check next to each characteristic listed in the descriptions. When you have read each characteristic for each of the Nine Points, go back and see where you find the most checks. Also note the numbers to each side of that Point. These Points might be influencing you as well. Look also at your patterns of behavior when you're responding to stress and strong feelings of happiness and security.

I would offer a caution about using checklists and tests, however.

You are on a spiritual journey. Being an educator, I believe in using resources such as tests and checklists to provide information, but the Enneagram and the Twelve Steps are about much more than mere information for the mind to use. As a spiritual director, I am deeply convinced that spiritual growth does not happen at the level of head information only. This is helpful, but a checklist or Enneagram test that suggests you operate out of a specific Point is not necessarily a message directly from God.

On the life journey of growth and maturing, it is your responsibility and privilege to observe yourself. You invite your Higher Being, your God, to help you look honestly at who you really are. It is not for others to label you. Do not allow others to tell you how to walk the Twelve Steps or what your Enneagram Point is. You can share with others, but do not forfeit your own inner work to anyone. Only you know yourself clearly at your deepest levels. Others can suggest, if you ask them to do so, but this is *your work*.

ABOUT THE ONE

FIGURE 6

POINT ONE

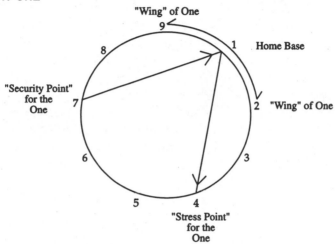

The name the One is called:
    Perfectionist (Palmer)
    Reformer (Riso)
    Need to Be Perfect (Rohr)
    Angry Virtue (Naranjo)
    Inspector (Beesing, Nogosek, O'Leary)

What grabs the One's attention:
    Right and wrong

The One's trait, obsession, defect:
    Anger (resentment), perfectionism

What the One avoids:
    Anger

How the One Pays Attention
    Ones focus on what is right or wrong in a situation, an idea, and in

the actions of others. Ones focus on the error to be corrected, seeing themselves responsible to correct it.

Ones also judge themselves in terms of right and wrong. They continually monitor themselves with what Palmer calls an "internal critic." Their constant self-monitoring is also called "judging mind." Their self-judgment is as harsh as their judgment of others.

It is interesting though that Ones can have what is called a "divided house." Ones try so hard to be good, but they can have a type of mechanism inside them that works like a "trapdoor release." Though so good, and while valuing goodness, they can live two lives, unaware that they are holding standards for others that they don't practice themselves.

Ones can repress their own impulses and desires. They can be very hard on themselves in their efforts to be not only good but perfect. In the name of work, doing the "right thing," Ones delay their own right to pleasure. They can be terribly critical of themselves and compare themselves with others. This criticality and internal repression can often result in anger and harsh, insensitive criticism of others.

To others, Ones can appear to be very angry people, yet Ones would be the first to deny that they're angry. Because Ones feel that it is not good to be angry, they are not in touch with the extent of their own anger. As they contain their anger, it turns into resentment, resentment toward others for not "doing good" or for not "doing good" as well as they should. If Ones do come in touch with their anger, they can justify it as legitimate because the other person is "doing wrong." Their own personal anger is justified because it is for a "righteous cause."

For Ones, other people gain value or inherent worthiness by being good and doing good. This is a hard place to be because perfectionism becomes an all-consuming, driving force. For Ones, perfectionism can become such a trap that they are unable to function, which leads to even more self-criticism. This hits at a deep level because Ones have learned that they gain their worthiness by being good.

How Being a One Can Affect Personal Behavior

Ones live with a relentless inner critic who is always affecting their self-esteem.

Ones develop the habit of ignoring their own needs and their right to experience personal pleasure.

Ones usually experience eruptions of their dark side through sexuality or aggression.

Ones experience a lot of worry.

Because Ones focus on correct detail, which impairs their productivity and ability to take action, they receive a great deal of criticism from others.

How the One Is Perceived by Others

Because Ones appear superior and critical, those around Ones often feel defensive, alienated, or punished.

Ones can be viewed as intense, experienced, and as having a reduced potential for enjoyment. They can experience within themselves a reduced potential for enjoyment.

Ones can experience intimacy as a source of tension because of their need to avoid showing their weakness or darker or needy side.

When actively angry, Ones can dredge up old events and feelings, lashing out at others with no forgiveness.

When Ones sense that others are struggling, making an effort, or working with good intentions, they can be very responsive.

Security and Stress Points: Seven and Four

If you have not yet determined whether you use the One as a "habit of mind," look again at Figure 6. The arrows in this figure indicate the directions Ones move when feeling secure or stressed.

Security Point Seven:

To see Ones' Security Point, follow the arrow to Point Seven (Figure 6). When happy, when drawing upon personal strengths, Ones observe themselves living with the higher aspects of Point Seven. When Ones experience themselves as more secure, as stronger in themselves, they have the psychic strength to swim against the flow of the arrow, to grow and reach to the higher aspects of the Seven. This also enhances their lives as they experience living with higher aspects of their own Point.

When growing and moving to the higher aspects of the Seven, Ones become more accepting of imperfections, their own and others'.

When working well and feeling secure, Ones are optimistic, playful, and relaxed.

Ones also become adept at working with things and with relationships as part of an ongoing process requiring give-and-take.

There does remain in discussion, too, the theory that individuals, when experiencing personal stress, will draw upon the lower aspects of the Security Point as a resource. For Ones, this is the Seven. If you think you might be a One, look at the higher and lower aspects of Point Seven.

Stress Point Four:
Refer to Figure 6 and follow the arrow from Point One to Point Four; this is Ones' Stress Point. When experiencing what they perceive as excessive pressure, Ones draw upon the lower aspects of Point Four. They coast, so to speak, along the arrow to another, safer space.

In this stress space, Ones give up and lose objectivity. They become depressed and unable to act. The experience is that of being caught in self-pity. Ones become overanxious and are unable to move beyond this.

Again, I remind you that there does remain in discussion the theory that when individuals are experiencing security, they can also draw upon the higher aspects of their Stress Point. Follow the arrow to the Four and read the higher aspects of this Point to better understand Ones.

The Side Points Wings: Nine and Two
When considering the influence of the sides of Point One, read the entire descriptions of both sides, those at Point Nine and those at Point Two. Honestly observe yourself and your patterns. If you have patterns that run you, you need to let them go. If you have patterns that you use in a healthy, wholesome way, then own this too.

The Basic Instincts (Subtypes)
AA and Twelve Step literature talk about basic emotions and habits of behavior that center around fear, anger, harms and hurts. You will examine these later on in the chapter that focuses on Step Four. Your responses depend upon the influence of your basic instincts. Palmer, Rohr, and Riso have done extensive research in this area, though they refer to the instincts as your "subtypes."

There are three areas of subtypes: 1) There is the need for one-on-one relationships, one-on-one intimacy, and sexuality connections. 2) There is the need for social or relational instinct. 3) There is the instinct for self-preservation. Usually, a person operates primarily out of one of these, though the others are also present. At times, a shift in life may cause the person to operate primarily out of another subtype for a period of time.

The important issue is to know yourself, to know your motives, to understand those instincts that are so deep down that you have learned to depend upon them at a very automatic level. If you don't look, you let them continue their influence, unbridled and unassisted by the light of truth.

One-on-one Instinct/Subtype: Jealousy

For Ones, the one-on-one instinct or subtype takes a form of jealousy. Ones operating out of this instinct monitor their mates' actions. They critically judge the relationship between themselves and their mate and what occurs within this relationship.

Social Instinct/Subtype: Nonadaptable

Ones operating out of this subtype can appear to be nonadaptable. This can look like rigidity and comes from confusion between their personal desires and their need to align with what they believe to be the "correct" position.

Self-preservation Instinct/Subtype: Anxious (Worried)

Ones operating out of this subtype or instinct live with worry, concerned that they are not perfect or right enough. They are very sensitive; they even wonder if they deserve to survive. They are afraid they will make a mistake and even jeopardize their very survival.

When the One Can Finally Surrender

Ones know powerlessness and are ready to surrender when they experience extreme anxiety attacks, so much so that they feel crippled, unable to function spiritually, emotionally, and possibly physically. When they experience their body failing them, Ones can no longer continue with the drive and tension of their own patterns. They develop real physical disorders that are rooted in psychological tension, and they know these disorders can be deadly if they're not addressed.

Ones know powerlessness and are ready to surrender when they are trapped in bouts of substance abuse. They do this to escape their internal critic, to find some peace. Substances can be of a wide variety, including food, alcohol, prescription or nonprescription medications, or drugs.

ABOUT THE TWO

FIGURE 7

POINT TWO

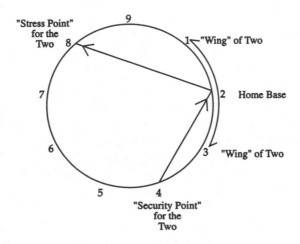

The name the Two is called:
Giver (Palmer)
Helper (Riso)
Need to Be Needed (Rohr)
Egocentric Generosity (Naranjo)
Assistant (Beesing, Nogosek, and O'Leary)

What Grabs the Two's attention:
Getting personal approval by meeting others' needs, by being selfless

The Two's trait, obsession, defect:
Pride, false love (I can meet your needs.)

What the Two avoids:
Their own needs.

How the Two Pays Attention

Twos take pride in the fact that they are really helpful and necessary for others. For Twos, relationships are all-important.

Twos believe that they can merge with the other person, or even move from group to group. They "alter" themselves, doing an emotional shift in order to gain acceptance and love from the persons they perceive as "significant others."

Twos have "feeling antennas" that make them pay attention to moods and feelings of others, as a type of interpersonal radar.

Twos can be very manipulative; they know how to form an alliance with those who have power. They can also maneuver others into liking them.

Twos have an extensive need to be needed, so they control by being helpful. They give; they help. They know how to meet the needs of others, but they also expect something in return—and they become very angry if they don't get it.

Twos can demonstrate extensive hysteria, anger, and mood shifts if they feel ignored or rejected. They have extensive needs for proofs and gestures of love.

Twos can engage in "triangulation." They often serve as mediators or messengers between opposing people or sides. They make the assumption that they can facilitate better than the warring parties can directly. This also endears them to each party.

Twos can present two separate "personas" or ways of being. They can be very seductive or very good and pure. This is sometimes discussed as the "madonna/whore" persona. They seduce, using sexual attention from the other person as a guarantee of approval.

Twos experience real anxiety when they try to feel their genuine feelings. They are risking rejection, but they still hunger to develop a freedom of their own will. They need to learn to shift inside themselves to observe what is going on within.

The "pride" of Twos is that they feel, "I can help you. I can know and meet your needs. I don't need anyone, but others need me."

Twos need to develop the virtue of humility. They need to embody the right amount of help for others, with no expectation of return.

The humility of Twos can also be that they learn to recognize their own needs, that they have needs, and that having needs is all right.

How Being a Two Can Affect Personal Behavior

Twos can experience a confusing, multiple sense of themselves and who they are.

They parcel themselves out on a regular basis to such an extent that they lose a sense of their own needs.

How the Two Is Perceived by Others

In new relationships, Twos flatter their partners' needs, but later they can feel controlled by their partners' will. They can be frustrated with a strong desire for freedom.

Twos can demonstrate hysterical outbursts of anger that are very hard for others to take.

Twos experience a conflict between dependence and independence. They present themselves as dependent in order to be irresistible, but they want their independence and the freedom to do what they please.

Twos can do a lot of complaining to show how much they are owed. When they give, they expect to get back in return. This can anger others.

Twos' involvement in triangulation (three-way communication) allows them to feel involved, but their real relationships become confusing.

Security and Stress Points: Four and Eight

If you have not yet determined whether you use the Two as a habit of mind, look again at Figure 7. Note the Security and Stress Points to see if any of these characteristics fit your patterns.

Security Point Four:

To see the Twos' Security Point, follow the arrow to Point Four. When happy, when drawing upon the Twos' strengths, Twos observe themselves living with the higher aspects of Point Four. When Twos experience themselves as more secure, as stronger in themselves, they have the psychic strength to swim against the flow of the arrow, to grow and reach to the higher aspects of the Four. This also enhances their lives as they experience living with higher aspects of their own Point.

When growing and moving to the higher aspects of the Four, Twos become less dependent; they rely more on their own strengths. They become able to recognize their own needs.

Twos grow to accept the reality that they are lovable completely apart from any service they provide for anyone.

There does remain in discussion, too, the theory that when experiencing personal stress, individuals also draw upon the lower aspects of the Security Point as a resource. For Twos, this is the Four. If you think you might be a Two, look at the higher and lower aspects of Point Four.

Stress Point Eight:

To see Twos' Stress Point, follow the arrow to Point Eight. When experiencing what they perceive as excessive pressure, this is where Twos draw upon the lower aspects of Point Eight. They coast, so to speak, along the arrow to another, safer space.

Twos react in a hostile and vengeful way when they feel unappreciated or scorned.

If Twos do not own their own feelings and frustrations, they become angry and hysterically aggressive.

Again, I would remind the reader that there does remain in discussion the theory that when individuals experience security, they can also draw upon the higher aspects of their Stress Point. Follow the arrow to the Eight, and read the higher aspects of this Point to understand the Two a little better.

The Side Points (Wings): One and Three

In considering the influence of the sides, read the entire descriptions of Point One and Point Three. Observe yourself and your patterns honestly. If you have patterns that run you, this is something to let go of. If you have patterns that you use in a healthy, wholesome way, then own this too.

The Basic Instincts (Subtypes)

One-on-one Instinct/Subtype: Seductive/Aggressive

Twos who operate out of the one-on-one subtype more than the other subtypes use seduction to entice and draw others to themselves.

Twos use aggression to get into others' spaces for contact. Twos push and find that aggression successfully overcomes many obstacles for contact when other strategies fail.

Social Instinct/Subtype: Ambitious

Twos look for association with powerful people as a source of their connectedness, protection, and identity. This association serves as an assurance of their status within the group.

Self-preservation Instinct/Subtype: Me-First (Privileged)

Twos hate to stand in line because they are afraid there will not be enough left for them.

Twos become angry when they are left out. They will maneuver themselves to the head of the line to take care of themselves.

When the Two Can Finally Surrender

Twos are ready to change their patterns and surrender to future growth when they can see that their way is not working anymore.

Twos move toward surrender when they look at how much of their lives have been invested in pleasing others for self-serving reasons. They begin to see how they have performed every day to meet the needs of others, while neglecting to care genuinely for themselves.

Twos live supporting others emotionally. Twos who are moving toward surrender develop a desire to find their real self, often to such an extent that they make themselves miserable. This can be stressful for those around them, but it is healthy for the twos.

Twos who are ready to change accept the fact that they have needs, that they experience frustrations with relationship issues because of significant inner and outer conflicts.

Twos frequently suffer from illnesses, including migraines and asthma.

ABOUT THE THREE

FIGURE 8

POINT THREE

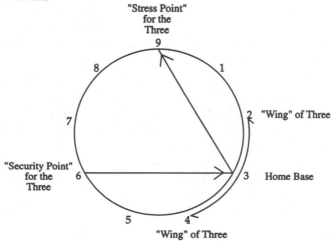

The name the Three is called:
Performer (Palmer)
Status Seeker (Riso)
Need to Succeed (Rohr)
Success Through Appearances (Naranjo)
Administrator (Beesing, Nogosek, and O'Leary)

What grabs the Three's attention:
Vanity, getting approval for job or success by being effective

The Three's trait, obsession, defect:
Self-deception, vanity

What the Three avoids:
Failure

How the Three Pays Attention
The Threes' sense of image and what they pay attention to are one

and the same. This is called identification. Threes become whatever it is they do.

Image for Threes translates as looking good according to the requirements of tasks to be done. They develop a pseudo, false self.

Threes are the ideal "doers" of projects. They work to earn love and acceptance by performing, by doing well and succeeding.

The defect of Threes is called deceit because of their level of self-deception. It has nothing to do, however, with consciously intending to deceive or lie. The deceit of Threes is a profound, serious deception of themselves. All individuals can practice self-deceit, but Threes aggressively package and market their value to others instead of knowing their intrinsic worth.

They pay attention, focusing on the tasks to accomplish. They use their leisure time to "network" or to accomplish their tasks well.

Threes focus on competition. They concentrate most or all of their attention on their single goal or project(s).

Threes are very "other referenced" instead of focusing interiorly, or upon their own needs and desires. They are dedicated to some future self-empowerment, outer task, or success.

Threes can be depended upon for efficiency and for their ability to handle pressure.

Threes become impatient when a project appears to be impeded. They can be very inattentive to the feelings of others, appearing to shift their own feelings as they perceive this to be effective. They can block their own feelings by focusing upon the task or project at hand.

The thought pattern of Threes is called "polyphasic"; Threes can process many activities and thoughts at the same time.

How Being a Three Can Affect Personal Behavior

Threes have a real self-deception about their own real needs and feelings.

They experience an incompleteness that drives them to move on to new tasks.

They know a deep fear as an anxiety that comes from nowhere and needs to be chased away by projects.

The impatience they show when differences are seen as obstructions to their goals can wear them out and push others away.

Threes need much admiration and attention. When deprived of

this, they can experience desperation, panic, loss, and the lower aspects of their own Point as well as those of their Stress Point, the Nine Point.

How the Three Is Perceived by Others

Threes can convey an intimacy with others because they sense what is expected, but at the same time, some report that they are aware they are performing a role.

In intimate relationships Threes are concerned with external appearances and accomplishments rather than depth of feeling.

Security and Stress Points: Six and Nine

If you have not yet determined whether you use the Three as a habit of mind, refer to the graph of the Enneagram and the arrows in Figure 8. Note the Security and Stress Points to see if any of these characteristics fit your patterns.

Security Point Six:

To see Threes' Security Point, follow the arrow to Point Six. When happy, when drawing upon the strengths of their own Point, this is where Threes observe themselves living with the higher aspects of Point Six. When Threes experience themselves as more secure, stronger in themselves, they have the psychic strength to swim against the flow of the arrow, to grow and reach to the higher aspects of the Six. This also enhances their lives as they experience living with higher aspects of their own Point.

Threes in security remain loyal to their best self and their friends. They learn to live with some healthy doubt and humility. They can become able to let themselves feel these feelings and many others. Threes become free within themselves, to view themselves as persons apart from their roles. They live more concretely, moving down to earth as human beings.

There does remain in discussion, too, the theory that when experiencing personal stress, individuals also draw upon the lower aspects of the Security Point as a resource. For Threes, this is the Six. If you think you might be a Three, look at the higher and lower aspects of Point Six.

Stress Point Nine:

To see Threes' Stress Point, follow the arrow to Point Nine. When Threes perceive themselves to be experiencing excessive pressure, they draw upon the lower aspects of Point Nine. They coast, so to speak, along the arrow to another, safer space.

At this Point Threes give up their efficiency. They find themselves dawdling in order to avoid conflicts. Threes become self-hostile, self-hating, and forgetful of their goals and purpose.

Again, I would remind the reader that there does remain in discussion the theory that when individuals experience security, they also can draw upon the higher aspects of their Stress Point. Follow the arrow to the Nine, and read the higher aspects of this point to understand Threes a little better.

The Side Points (Wings): Four and Two

In considering the influence of the sides of your Point, read the entire descriptions of the two sides: Point Four and Point Two. Observe yourself and your patterns honestly. If you have patterns that run you, let go of them. If you have patterns that you use in a healthy, wholesome way, own this too.

The Basic Instincts/Subtypes

One-on-one Instinct/Subtype: Masculinity/Femininity

The one-on-one issue for Threes is the issue of the image of masculinity or femininity.

For Threes living predominately out of this subtype, living instinctually from this level, having a sexually appealing image is important. For Threes, being aware of performing a role effectively is directly related to their personal value. This need to project a winning sexual image masks, or conceals, for themselves as well as for others, their very deep confusion about themselves.

Social Instinct/Subtype: Prestige

The social (small group) subtype for Threes is prestige. Threes are preoccupied with presenting a good social image; they alter themselves to assume what they believe to be the valued characteristics of whichever group they are connecting with at the time.

The Three also prefers to be in the position to lead the group.

Self-preservation Instinct/Subtype: Security

The self-preservation subtype focuses on the Threes' need to have security. For Threes, money and material ownership is essential in order to reduce their anxiety for personal survival. Threes work hard in order to have the money and the status that would appear to provide for their security.

When the Three Can Finally Surrender

When Threes experience some sort of enforced slowdown due to illness, physical breakdown, personal loss, or job loss, they find that their feelings begin to surface.

These feelings can create overwhelming problems for them, especially if they are at a place in their life when they feel powerless and ready to surrender. As children, Threes were prized for achieving rather than for being themselves. They were the best at activities that were valued by the people they held as significant. As adults, Threes find that their life experiences are different. They can perhaps find the personal courage to live "listening to their own drummer." Their journeys are finally ready to begin for real.

If you are a Three and you are now experiencing overwhelming frustration and loss, you might be ready to walk the Twelve Step journey.

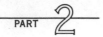
ABOUT THE FOUR

FIGURE 9

POINT FOUR

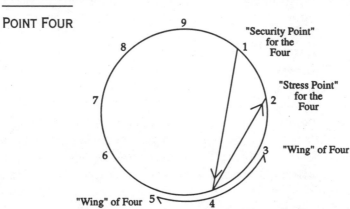

The name the Four is called:
Tragic-Romantic (Palmer)
Artist (Riso)
Need to Be Special (Rohr)
Seeking Happiness Through Pain (Naranjo)
Author (Beesing, Nogosek, and O'Leary)

What grabs the Four's attention:
Longing for the attractive, seeing themselves as special, the distant is better, the worst is here

The Four's trait, obsession, defect:
Envy, dissatisfaction, melancholy

What the Four avoids:
The mundane, the common

How the Four Pays Attention

Fours have a special investment and aptitude for using their feeling "antennae." They pay attention to the moods and feelings of others using a type of personal radar. They are not feeling with the other. It is as if they are standing back from the other, yet in a subtle way they are feeling superior because they can sense the feelings.

Fours are always longing for the special, unavailable object (a special person to love, the ideal job). They see themselves as special.

Fours live with an ongoing lamentation for what is "missing." Theirs is a quality of pining for the missing, the not-present, the past, the future, the absent, the hard to get. This preoccupies them to such an extent that they are unable to be productive.

When Fours walk, many times it is with a swish, as if wearing a special great cloak.

Four experience a "push-pull" in life. They feel negative about what is here and positive about what is distant or "not yet."

Fours like to keep life at a safe distance from themselves. They focus on feelings, especially upon sadness.

Theirs is a life of extremes. They prefer intensity in life, anything that is not the common, the everyday. Life is better either as suffering or total fulfillment, as "lows or highs."

Fours can demonstrate extreme mood swings from depression to hyperactivity. They can be depressed, withdrawing in search of meaning. They can appear hyperactive and not depressed in order to get meaning from activities or love affairs quickly. They can experience a variety of change within themselves as inner mood swings. They can appear externally normal while secretly maintaining an option of being open for suicide.

For Fours, depression is a frequent mood. Their lament is often, "If only, if only." For them life is like a deep dark pit. There is no hope, no help for them, even if it is offered. For Fours melancholy is a bittersweet yearning that comes from their sense of loss at not gaining the impossible. This sadness makes it easy for them to call up imagery and metaphor and connection with distant things.

Fours have a unique temperamental sensitivity. They abhor the "common" present, the "now." For them, "The best is distant, the worst is here."

Theirs is a pain amplified by an addiction to suffering.

They often experience a jealousy that consumes them toward those with fulfillment.

Fours have a capacity to use rage as a biting sarcasm. They cut others down as if to "even the score," while at the same time they are filled with self-criticism that they turn inward.

Fours see themselves as "special." Ordinary rules are not meant for them. The rules are for them to "get away with."

Fours like to "go for the best!" Their body often reflects their self image, so they usually are slim, and can be anorexic.

How Being a Four Can Affect Personal Behavior

Fours suffer extensively because their perception feeds a dissatisfied view of life. Life is not satisfactory. They experience anger with life as it is.

They are dominated by fluctuating feelings of pain, depression, devastation, disdain, drama, deviancy, and feelings that they don't quite fit in. They experience themselves as misfits and as misunderstood.

They suffer because, when they do get what they want, even this becomes common, boring, and undesirable. They can't sustain relationships or the work of remaining on the chosen life path.

They experience an addiction to pain and suffering.

The choking envy of Fours can cripple them in their relationships with others.

How the Four Is Perceived by Others

For others, Fours' tendency to resist intimacy, to separate from them, is difficult to tolerate.

Fours are capable of a biting sarcasm that is very hard to take. When in this "space," Fours are resistant to looking at how they are treating others.

Fours' "on again, off again," "rubber-band" relationship pattern caused by their shifts of mood can be very difficult to experience.

Others can feel guilty for failing to be "enough" for a Four.

Others feel hurt and anger when they experience rejection by a Four.

It can be difficult for others to cope with a Four's endless life crises.

Security and Stress Points: One and Two

If you have not yet determined if you are using the Four as a habit of mind, perhaps you could look at the graph of the Enneagram in Figure 9 and look at the arrows to see if any of the low or high aspects of these Points might be in yourself.

Security Point One:

To see the Fours' Security Point, follow the arrow to Point One. This is where, when happy, when drawing upon the strengths of the Fours' own Point, Fours observe themselves living with the higher aspects of Point One. When Fours experience themselves as more secure, as stronger in themselves, they have the psychic strength to swim against the flow of the arrow, to grow and reach to the higher aspects of the One. This also enhances their lives as they experience living with higher aspects of their own Point.

When drawing upon the higher aspects of Point One, Fours become comfortably assertive. They are able to act consistently with a delight in working to serve, to change themselves, their work, and their relationships for the better. Fours lose their feelings of inferiority. Rather than feeling they have to get busy in order to feel better, they become busy at activities they choose mindfully and deliberately. They become able to go peacefully inside their feelings, and be present to themselves and their own lives. They become secure in themselves and are able to remain in the present, helping, but also able to say no.

There does remain in discussion, too, the theory that when experiencing personal stress, individuals also draw upon the lower aspects of the Security Point as a resource. For the Fours this is the One. I would suggest that if you think you might be a Four, look at the higher and lower aspects of Point One.

Stress Point Two

To see the Fours' Stress Point, follow the arrow to Point Two. This is where, when experiencing what the Fours perceive as excessive pressure, they draw upon the lower aspects of Point Two. They coast, so to speak, along the arrow to another, safer space.

Fours in stress feel trapped. They do what others want. They can't say no. They look and feel "wimpy." They are too dependent upon others and very "doleful." They become helpless and cling to others to take care of their emotional and physical needs if they can find others willing to do so.

Again, I would remind the reader that there does remain in discussion the theory that when individuals experience security, they also can draw upon the higher aspects of their Stress Point. Follow the arrow to the Two and read the higher aspects of this Point to understand the Four a little better.

The Side Points (Wings): Three and Five

In considering the influence of the sides of your Point, read the entire descriptions of the two sides, Point Three and Point Five. Observe yourself and your patterns honestly. If you have patterns that run you, this is something to let go of. If you have patterns that you use in a healthy, wholesome way, then own this too.

The Basic Instincts (Subtypes)

One-on-one Instinct/Subtype: Competitive/Hateful

Fours living out of the sexual (one-on-one) subtype operate by exclusivity. These Fours are always competing to get the exclusive attention of someone. They are always focused upon getting the respect of those they consider to be the "best" people.

Social Instinct/Subtype: Shame

Fours in this subtype are filled with shame. They operates in ways to reinforce the belief that they are not measuring up to the group standards. For them, the group is made up of those they consider to be important or worthy of their attention.

Self-preservation Instinct/Subtype (Survival): Dauntless, Reckless

The dauntless recklessness of Fours is around the issue of their personal survival. Fours in this subtype repeat patterns for years at a time. They feel secure by recreating the possibility of loss through their reckless actions. It is as if they are spitting in the face of fear. They find excitement in playing on the edge of disaster.

When the Four Can Finally Surrender

Fours become ready for Step One, to surrender what has worked for them until now, when they want to break the bondage of their depression. They begin to understand that the depression is coming from a childhood anger turned inward, and they are trapped in it.

When Fours observe how their intense mood swings jeopardize their own lives and impact the lives of others, they become ready to let go of them. This usually happens as the mood swings affect those who are what they consider to be most dear to them.

At the crux of the issues for the Fours is a sense of enduring loss. This could have been due to a literal abandonment, a divorce, a death.

It could even have been caused by seemingly benign parental neglect or inconsistency. It could be caused by experiences of cruel inconsistency. What is critical for Fours is that they become tired of how much they have held on to this "loss" in their life. It doesn't work for them anymore, but they don't know how to let go of how they are. They experience powerlessness. They becomes desperate.

Fours are ready to surrender when they experience a desperate desire to find their real selves. When they find that they really want to continue a relationship and that what they're doing isn't working for them, they are open to getting help.

Some Fours find a readiness to surrender when their bodies intervene. When they experience illness such as psychosomatic disorders due to their repressed needs, these illnesses impede their goals, and they begin to want help. Some illnesses that debilitate Fours are migraines, asthma, and anxiety attacks.

ABOUT THE FIVE

FIGURE 10

POINT FIVE

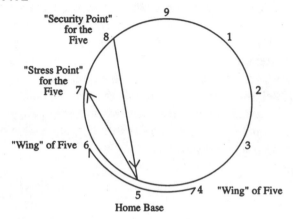

The name the Five is called:
> Observer (Palmer)
> Thinker (Riso)
> Need to Perceive (Rohr)
> Seeking Wholeness Through Isolation (Naranjo)
> Sage (Beesing, Nogosek, and O'Leary)

What grabs the Five's attention:
> Looking to see what others want from them. A self-perception that they can see more clearly than others.

The Five's trait, obsession, defect:
> Avarice, greed, stinginess

What the Five avoids:
> Emptiness

How the Five Pays Attention

Fives live in a type of stance where they are looking outward to others, observing, thinking, scanning in a self-protective mode as if asking, "What do others want from me?"

This is a fear-based point. Fives are afraid to feel and frequently dampen and reduce their feelings. They delay feeling so that they can reflect later on the emotions and events.

Fives take an "observer" stance in life. They live with a type of disassociation (detachment) from life. They do not like to be visible, so they avoid situations of competition, self-promotion, and demonstrations of love and hate.

Fives feel secretly superior and aloof from others.

They like to stand back and analyze, making mental constructs of interactions in order to feel connected with others.

They like to engage in mental "mapping" (Palmer), studying systems and patterns of how things connect with each other. This helps them to feel they are connected with others.

Fives engage in something called "compartmentalizing." They withdraw, detaching in their minds by separating and segmenting things in time. They use an internal frame of reference to control people, places, and things. They do this in order to avoid being trapped or intruded upon by others.

Fives construct a type of mental castle to protect their space.

The Fives' principal defect or passion is to hold on to ideas in order to be sure they are right. They tend to hold on to information and to avoid sharing it. They do this not to be selfish, but because they need to know it is correct before releasing it or sharing, just in case others would criticize or hurt them.

Fives see themselves as frugal, but this is really an attempt to limit their needs and wants to a minimum so that they can avoid dependency upon others. They select independence instead of satisfaction in the realm of the emotions and connection with others.

Fives can appear to be very rigid. They are actually thinking through in advance of action in order to have some predictability in life. They depend upon their knowledge and information to explain life. For Fives it is not life's experiences that are important but the reflection upon them.

Fives have a type of pride where they confuse their nonattachment and noninvolvement with what is really an emotional shutdown to keep out pain. Real nonattachment is the openness to having a full range of feelings available to oneself to accept any impressions that come, and to be able to "let go" of them freely.

How Being a Five Can Affect Personal Behavior

Fives experience a deep sense of isolation from their own feelings. It is extremely difficult for them to express what they are experiencing in the present here and now. It is difficult for them to know their inner feelings.

Fives respond to inner fear by withdrawing from life into a pattern of reducing even vital needs to a minimum.

Fives often live in quiet desperation with feelings of loneliness and inadequacy.

Fives know that they have failed to act many times. They feel they have missed opportunities in life because they held back, protecting their time and space.

Fives experience much threat in life because they experience requests from others as demands upon them. This is threatening and leads to rage deep inside them.

How the Five Is Perceived by Others

Those who care about the Five can feel frozen out by the privacy needs of the Five. Fives also tend to avoid conflict so that the work of confrontation falls on the other person. This can lead to resentment and anger in the other person.

What Fives see as their self-control can be experienced by others as if they are hoarding their time, their space, their energy, their "self."

Fives' apparent secrecy and stance of not revealing themselves can be a source of conflict for others.

Fives can become very jealous and even more protective of what they value, especially if they feel their "important other" will leave.

Fives feel most intensely when alone. Their connection is mental rather than emotional. In their relationships Fives need clear limits as to the time and energy required. Their sexuality and one-to-one relationships are often expressed through nonverbal communication, symbols, and gestures. They need their significant others to understand and accept this in them.

Security and Stress Points: Eight and Seven

If you have not yet determined if you are using the Five as a habit of mind, perhaps you could look at the graph of the Enneagram in Figure 10 and look at the arrows of the Stress and Security Points.

Security Point: Eight

To see Fives' Security Point, follow the arrow to Point Eight. This is where, when happy, Fives are drawing upon the strengths of their own Point. Fives observe themselves living as a more secure person. They feel stronger in themselves. They have the psychic strength to swim against the flow of the arrow, to grow and reach to the higher aspects of the Eight. This also enhances their lives as they experience living with higher aspects of their own Point.

When Fives experience the higher aspects of the Eight, there is an experience of personal power. Fives let go of their fear and their reservations. They become able to make their ideas happen. They become able to express and to carry out their ideas. They become able to be assertive and self-reliant but comfortable with others as well. They become more comfortable with their bodies. Fives do not live as much as self-protective persons operating out of their heads. Rather, they become more integrated, focused, and secure people.

There does remain in discussion, too, the theory that when experiencing personal stress, individuals also draw upon the lower aspects of the Security Point as a resource. For Fives this is the Eight. If you think you might be a Five, look at the higher and lower aspects of Point Eight.

Stress Point: Seven

To see the Fives' Stress Point, follow the arrow to Point Seven. This is where, when experiencing what Fives perceive as excessive pressure, they draw upon the lower aspects of Point Seven. They coast, so to speak, along the arrow to another, safer, more protective space.

Fives in stress are afraid and feel overwhelmed. They protect by isolating themselves from others and from the reality they are trying to avoid.

They disconnect into a fantasy world and say to themselves, "I'm enjoying the stimulus in my life right now." "I'm so busy, I don't have time to pay attention to that stuff." They stay out of touch with relationships and their feelings by hiding in the realm of stimuli: multiple ideas, food, drugs, and excessive activity. They become very cerebral to the extent that they are out of touch with the basic needs of their bodies and their feelings. They can then experience even more stress. They become physically exhausted as they become angrier and more desperate. They move even further back into the back row of the observer stance.

Again, I would remind the reader that there does remain in discussion the theory that when individuals experience security, they also can draw upon the higher aspects of their Stress Point. Follow the arrow to the Seven and read the higher aspects of this Point to understand Fives a little better.

The Side Points (Wings): Four and Six

In considering the influence of the sides of your Point, read the entire descriptions of the two sides, Point Four and Point Six. Observe yourself and your patterns honestly. If you have patterns that run you, this is something to let go of. If you have patterns that you use in a healthy, wholesome way, then own this too.

The Basic Instincts (Subtypes):

One-on-one Instinct/Subtype: Sharing Confidences, Secretive

For Fives the one-on-one relationship is a bond greatly founded upon confidentiality. Fives put more confidence in what they experiences as nonverbal sexual communication than the more public form of interpersonal communication. Fives experience a personal, inner intensity when they have this secret bond.

Social Instinct/Subtype: Totems in Social Arena

Fives in this subtype need to feel that they are connected in a secure way to the significant, key people of the "group." It is important to them to feel they are valued for what they might offer as a resource. They value this special position as "prestige." They like to be called upon to give advice to the inner circle of the group. They will also be more inclined to accept advice from the key significant others.

Fives are content to seek meaningful expressions of life through understanding and gathering of symbols. They settle for these instead of the reality they represent. They might pursue scientific formulas, systems such as the Enneagram, or images of cultures they value such as art or literature.

Fives of this subtype might live very simply except for a major collection of some sort. Some Fives have been known to collect hundreds or even thousands of records, books, art of a certain type, as if this focus contributes to their worth as being all-wise, all-knowing, able to share if called upon.

Self-preservation Instinct/Subtype: Castle, Home

Fives of this subtype feel the need to have a special place where they can take refuge from what they see as an invading world. They live their lives with a preoccupation with control and protection of their own private, personal space. For some, this is a room or a home that is very aesthetically reduced. For others, this space is filled and they exert total control over it, which gives them a sense of being in charge, wise, and strong. Palmer refers to this as "a womb with a view."

When the Five Can Finally Surrender

Fives live with their feelings detached. The pattern that works for them has been to withdraw and accept whatever fate comes upon them. As young people, they might have experienced life as being physically or emotionally intrusive. They might have felt abandoned. Social relationships were difficult for them, so they insulated themselves from their fear. When Fives feel trapped by the withdrawal and fear patterns that have so far worked for them, when they can no longer tolerate the prison of their fear, they begin to be ready to take Step One.

When Fives realize the extent of their isolation and loneliness, how much they has been cut off from their feelings, their own bodies, and their relationships, Fives are ready to surrender to a newer, stronger life.

ABOUT THE SIX

FIGURE 11

POINT SIX

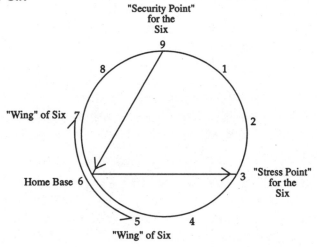

The name the Six is called:
Devil's Advocate (Palmer)
Loyalist (Riso)
Need for Security/Certainty (Rohr)
Persecuted Persecutor (Naranjo)
Facilitator (Beesing, Nogosek, and O'Leary)

What grabs the Six's attention:
Others' hidden motives, security in doing their duty

The Six's trait, obsession, defect:
Fear, doubt, cowardice

What the Six avoids:
Deviance, delinquency

How the Six Pays Attention

Individuals in the Six space usually expect the worst from others and from situations. It is easy for Sixes to see the "worst-case scenario." Palmer gives them the name the "Devil's Advocate." Their stance in life is a defensiveness based on fear. This serves them well to recognize real danger, when others are content to feel safe.

Sixes operate with a self-protective mechanism called "scanning" (Palmer). They use scanning to explain their inner sense of fear and doubt. They have a capacity for a hypervigilance and are continually scanning for danger in their environment and relationships. They can also exaggerate what they think they see.

Sixes can be hypersensitive to double messages, always trying to use their minds to figure out the route to safety.

Sixes have the capacity to see with a "third eye," a psychic sense. They can experience insights as impressions and visions. These insights help them see implications and inferences for the present and the future.

There are two subcategories unique to the Six Point, the Phobic Six, (backing off, afraid, full of fear) and the Counterphobic Six, (covering the fear by pushing themselves to act in spite of or against the fear). Phobic Sixes are trapped in place, afraid to act because of their fear. Counterphobic Sixes are full of fear, but they go so far as to put themselves in positions of danger in order to reduce their fear. They have to prove to themselves that they are able to do this.

Sixes can find themselves stuck in a pattern of procrastination. When they experience success, they become threatened, fearing criticism or hurt, so they jeopardize their success by delaying whatever "right action" needs to be done. Sixes fear success. When they do procrastinate, it is usually as an avoidance, a type of amnesia surrounding success. Sixes have a problem with authority. They can overtrust or undertrust authority figures. They surrender too much of their own personal authority, overvaluing a strong leader, guru, mentor, system, institution, or a group that will keep them safe. They can also act with rebellion against authority, sticking up for the underdog, risking harm to do what they believe is right, being suspicious of the motives and dictates of others.

Sixes also have a strong capacity for loyalty. They tend to enjoy surrounding themselves with people of like interests in a group or cause, and they seek influence with those in this group. They work for a cause or creative ideal with dedication and loyalty. They do not usually want rewards or notice for their efforts, and they work to avoid this.

Sixes can engage easily in projection. They assign to others their own doubts, and they mistrust others.

Because of their fear, Sixes try to avoid anger from others by not inflicting themselves on others.

Sixes can also be very warm, doing their duties and connecting with others in order to be assured of their goodwill.

This tendency to be suspicious of the motives of others, can make Sixes very uncomfortable if praised.

How Being a Six Can Affect Personal Behavior

Sixes can experience a profound frustration and confusion because of their procrastination. They can envision what they really want to do but can experience a profound inner incompleteness due to their ambivalence.

Sixes' difficulties with authority (as either oversubmission or defiance) can lead to profound inner conflicts, anxiety, and rage.

Sixes' hypervigilance, their overactive imagination, their misreading and mistrusting others, trap them. They are limited in their capacity to see enjoyable, even obvious, options and possibilities.

How the Six Is Perceived by Others

When Sixes make a commitment, whether to work, to a relationship, or to a group, they will usually remain in the commitment for long periods of time. Their sense of duty will lead them to follow through on any problems that may arise. When Sixes make a commitment, and the relationship continues, they can reduce their suspiciousness and become trusting of others. They will be loyal when hard times come, putting others' welfare before their own and enjoying others' success as their own. On the other hand, if Sixes do something wrong or become angry, they can attribute their feelings of guilt, or anger, to their partner or colleague. This can put excessive strain upon the relationship.

Security and Stress Points: Nine and Three

If you have not yet determined if you are using the Six as a habit of mind, perhaps you could look at the graph of the Enneagram in Figure 11 and look at the arrows.

Security Point: Nine

This is where, when happy, when drawing upon the strengths of their own Point, Sixes observe themselves living with the higher aspects of Point Nine. When Sixes experience themselves as more secure, as stronger in themselves, they have the psychic strength to swim against the flow of the arrow, to grow and reach to the higher aspects of the Nine. This also enhances their lives as they experience living with higher aspects of their own Point.

Sixes who feel secure are able to relax and are comfortable with themselves and with others. They are receptive to others and capable of great empathy.

There does remain in discussion, too, the theory that when experiencing personal stress, individuals also draw upon the lower aspects of the Security Point as a resource. If you think you might be a Six, look at the higher and lower aspects of Point Nine.

Stress Point: Three

To see the Sixes' Stress Point, follow the arrow to Point Three. This is where, when experiencing what Sixes perceive as excessive pressure, they draw upon the lower aspects of Point Three. They coast, so to speak, along the arrow to another, safer, more protective space.

Sixes in stress can become very scattered, engaging in frantic activity. They become suspicious of others' motives, and even paranoid about those who they think are thwarting what is important to them. They can become very aggressive, exhibiting a style of leadership that can seem close to authoritarian and rigid.

Again, I would remind the reader that there does remain in discussion the theory that when individuals experience security, they can also draw upon the higher aspects of the Stress Point. Follow the arrow to the Three, and read the higher aspects of this Point to understand Sixes a little better.

The Side Points (Wings): Five and Seven

In considering the influence of the sides of your Point, read the entire descriptions of the two sides, Point Five and Point Seven. Observe yourself and your patterns honestly. If you have patterns that run you, this is something to let go of. If you have patterns that you use in a healthy, wholesome way, then own this too.

The Basic Instincts (Subtypes)

One-on-one Instinct/Subtype: Strength and Beauty

The one-on-one relationship for Sixes presents itself as a preoccupation with strength and beauty. This comes from their need to have a sense of their own personal power over the other because they feel afraid. This can be as a falsely macho presentation of physical or mental strength, or the ability to affect the other sexually.

Social Instinct/Subtype (Group): Duty

Sixes in this subtype work to gain the loyalty of others, in order to be assured of safety to minimize their fear. They do this by adhering to the rules and the obligations for social behavior expected of them by their significant society, organization, or group.

Self-preservation Instinct/Subtype: Warmth

Sixes in this subtype present themselves as warm and friendly to others. They do this to be able to be assured of other people's affection. This protects them from potential hostility, so that their level of fear can be reduced.

When the Six Can Finally to Surrender

As children, some individual Sixes experienced punishment and humiliation by their parents, perhaps through unpredictable or erratic discipline. These Sixes may have experienced that they were on the weaker side without anyone to protect them. When they can see the extent to which they are continuing to let their fear and distrust control them, many Sixes seek help. They become ready to take Step One.

When Sixes observe that they are truly unable to be comfortable in relationships or with sexual activity, this can lead them to seek help.

When Sixes realize that a pattern is controlling them in regard to the inability to do work, complete projects, or hold a job, they may seek help.

Many Sixes surrender when they find their body developing psychosomatic disorders as a result of trying to handle the fear in their heads. When they see the extent to which they do not live in partnership with their emotions and their body, many are ready to take Step One.

ABOUT THE SEVEN

FIGURE 12

POINT SEVEN

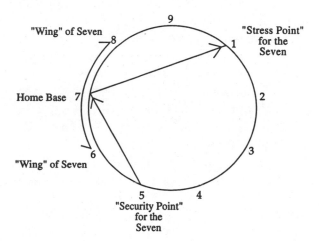

"Wing" of Seven — 8

9

"Stress Point" for the Seven — 1

Home Base 7

2

"Wing" of Seven — 6

3

5

4

"Security Point" for the Seven

The name the Seven is called:
   Planner or Epicure (Palmer)
   Generalist (Riso)
   Need to Avoid Pain (Rohr)
   Opportunistic Idealism (Naranjo)
   Optimist (Beesing, Nogosek, and O'Leary)

What grabs the Seven's attention:
   Pleasant options, happy optimism

The Seven's trait, obsession, defect:
   Gluttony, fraudulence

What the Seven avoids:
   Problems, pain

How the Seven Pays Attention
   Sevens are always looking at life with a lens "tinted" to filter out

pain. They look to pleasant options. A strategy they employ to do this is that they are regularly planning in their minds. This is good, in itself, but when employed habitually, it takes the form of a subtle mechanism to avoid reality. Sevens are looking to experience their next fascinating enterprise. By doing this, they escape the more boring or difficult present. If there is pain, they look the other way.

This is a fear Point as well, but Sevens cheerfully defuse their fear by mentally creating limitless possibilities.

Sevens are experts at keeping multiple options open at all times so as not to get stuck in intensity or intimacy. They don't have to be bored or hurt.

Sevens use rationalization. They use their minds to reframe experiences toward pleasure and away from pain. This is a problem, because by habitually responding in their minds, they ignore the option for integration with real feelings and needs.

Like Sixes, Sevens have a problem with authority. Their response to authority is to equalize it. They view bosses and leaders as equals. They figure out ways to get the authority person to do what they want.

Sevens are skilled at linking together different, unrelated parts of information. They generalize easily and quickly for much broader applications from their synergizing of ideas. They like the "juice" of this creative, new thought.

Sevens can appear very narcissistic and self-referencing. Their form of this is to reference everything from inside themselves. They operate out of relative values, regardless of the norms of the broader societies or groups to which they belong.

Sevens usually demonstrate a pattern of feeling superior and inferior in their relationships with others. They are continually assessing their position with others regarding recognition and support.

The trait of gluttony is attributed to Sevens. This can be a physical delight in pleasure and food, but it is a mental hunger as well. The bodily hunger of Sevens is for extremes in excitement and experience. Sevens are addicted to their own adrenaline, to have physical energy, adventure, and to use substances to feel high. They have a keen sensitivity and a high sense of taste for gourmet food.

The mental gluttony of Sevens is for the stimulation of ideas, theories, and systems. They learn quickly and broadly, but they flit mentally with their associations rather than allowing themselves to experience the implications of knowledge and systems for their lives. They don't like the discipline of in-depth extended study because they can "get the idea" a lot faster learning on their own—their way.

Sevens are charmers. By their pleasing personality, they raise the expectations of others and are liked by interesting people. Though they appears totally invested in others, when they do not need these people anymore, Sevens simply forget them. Palmer refers to this trait as "forgetting the forgotten lover's name."

How Being a Seven Can Affect Personal Behavior

Though being healthy is important to Sevens, they can experience overload in their bodies and their emotions. This would be the result of trying to keep the excitement going over time without balance.

Sevens who invest in pursuing their own immediate desires, jobs, and relationships can eventually experience an anxiety or depression as part of a loss of purpose.

They can experience conflict from their need to equalize authority when the authority resists their manipulation.

How the Seven Is Perceived by Others

The narcissism and self-centeredness of Sevens can make others feel that they don't really care. Others feel they can't depend on Sevens. On the other hand, Sevens can become very aggressive when they experience confrontation and recrimination. Sevens do not like to feel that they have failed.

The tendency to convey that they feel superior can weary others.

Sevens who do not keep commitments can cause pain for those who depend upon them. This can create conflicts at work, at home, or with the groups of which Sevens claim to be a part. Sevens can schedule a meeting, then cancel it or come late, forcing others to wait, because they filled their schedule with more interesting opportunities. Sevens can also quit a job, get a divorce, or abandon projects when the happiest options no longer appear in the forefront.

Because Sevens tend to minimize pain and deny reality, they appear to trivialize their experiences, life issues, and pain. Sevens can demonstrate great impatience with those who are emotionally dependent or with extensive needs. This can be painful for those incurring the wrath.

Because Sevens do not take the time to work out smaller conflicts or difficulties, they can stockpile them within. Eventually, they lash out in the present with a disproportionate rage fueled from these distant grievances.

Security and Stress Points: Five and One

If you have not yet determined if you are using the Seven as a habit of mind, look at the graph of the Enneagram in Figure 12 and look at the arrows. Note the Security and Stress Points to see if any of these characteristics fit your patterns.

Security Point: Five

This is where, when happy, when drawing upon the strengths of the Sevens' own Point, they observe themselves living with the higher aspects of Point Five. When Sevens experience themselves as more secure, as stronger in themselves, they have the psychic strength to swim against the flow of the arrow, to grow and reach to the higher aspects of the Five. This also enhances their lives as they experience living with higher aspects of their own Point.

Sevens who draw upon the higher gifts of the Five are still able to plan, but they are able to apply their plans. They are able to remain at projects, on jobs, in relationships, with dedication and focus. They are less hyperactive, more reflective, and more wisely interpersonal.

There does remain in discussion, too, the theory that when experiencing personal stress, individuals also draw upon the lower aspects of the Security Point as a resource. If you think you might be a Seven, look at the higher and lower aspects of Point Five.

Stress Point: One

To see Sevens' Stress Point, follow the arrow to Point One. This is where, when experiencing what Sevens perceive as excessive pressure, they draw upon the lower aspects of Point One. They coast, so to speak, along the arrow to another, safer, more protective space.

Sevens in stress experience extreme anger and self-righteous resentment. They can become very cynical, focusing on the imperfections in the situation or the relationship. When they begin to connect with their pain, this becomes an ongoing process that appears to them as a bottomless pit or interminable hell. Sevens in stress can lose all impressions of pleasant sweetness in their outlook and manner.

Again, I would remind the reader that there does remain in discussion the theory that when individuals experience security, they can also draw upon the higher aspects of their Stress Point. Follow the arrow to the One and read the higher aspects of this point to understand Sevens a little better.

The Side Points (Wings): Eight and Six

In considering the influence of the sides of your Point, read the entire descriptions of the two sides, Point Eight and Point Six. Observe yourself and your patterns honestly. If you have patterns that run you, this is something to let go of. If you have patterns that you use in a healthy, wholesome way, then own this too.

The Basic Instincts (Subtypes)

One-on-one Instinct/Subtype: Suggestibility

Sevens with this subtype live always open and eager for new experiences and ideas. They become heightened in their being through the force of their positive imagination. They will take on the ideas as truth quickly in their eager search for more stimulus, energy, "quick fixes," and heightened senses.

On a one-to-one basis, people important to Sevens are those who are "bringers of experience" for them. These people can share the Sevens' hunger and contribute to the Sevens' desire for new experiences, ideas, and positive energy.

Social Instinct/Subtype: Sacrifice (Martyr)

Sevens in this subtype are willing to accept limits in their lives. They are open to restrictions of their options if these are imposed because of their commitments to others. They can do this because they view the limitations as only temporary. In their view, the limitations will eventually bring them toward more positive future goals, interests, and stimuli.

Self-preservation Instinct/Subtype: "Like-Minded," Family

Sevens in this subtype like the security of belonging to a group of people who mirror their beliefs and interests. For these Sevens, a basic level of threat is reduced so that they can enjoy their extensive level of activities, mental activity, work, and relationships.

When the Seven Can Finally Surrender

As Sevens continue with their thirst for "more" in life, they find that eventually this thirst cannot be satiated. Especially if the reason is financial difficulty, they can find themselves experiencing deprivation and depression. This suffering will help them become ready to surrender.

It is highly possible for Sevens to experience a mid-life crisis when they see the discrepancy between their imagined expectations and what they have really done with their lives. This awareness can lead Sevens to be ready to change.

When they find they cannot commit to a relationship they are unable to complete tedious projects they really want to do, or when they realize addictions are controlling them, they become ready to surrender.

ABOUT THE EIGHT

FIGURE 13

POINT EIGHT

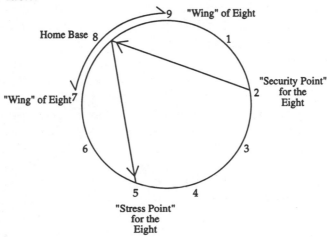

The name the Eight is called:
Boss (Palmer)
Leader (Riso)
Need to Be Against (Rohr)
Coming On Strong (Naranjo)
Champion (Beesing and O'Leary)

What grabs the Eight's attention:
Control, being just and strong

The Eight's trait, obsession, defect:
Lust, vengeance

What the Eight avoids:
Weakness

How the Eight Pays Attention

Eights' antennae go to being the controller in the situation, the relationship. They seem to have an internal question: "Who has the power, and will he be fair?" (Palmer). I say "antennae" because Eights are very intuitive people who depend upon their impressions of the space, gut instinct, and energy around them. This is based in their bodies. Eights are outwardly focused. They look to action and power for life.

Eights can practice dominance of others very easily. They do not see that this is what they are doing. This includes the people in their lives, their space, and their things.

Eights can be very self-righteous, judging situations as just or unjust, as "all or nothing" propositions. This is not the same "perfectionism" of Ones with an objective right and wrong outside of themselves. Eights can push themselves extensively when justice and truth are concerned, but it is because they feel responsible to act. They have a great capacity to remain dedicated until a project is completed, a wrong righted, the weak protected, and so forth.

Eights are very comfortable being aggressive and openly angry, or moving against others. Anger is seen as a protection and represents strength that requires the other's respect. They like intensity and conflict. They feel this is helpful for them as a tool to test the other's authenticity. This testing does not come from a position of strength, though Eights believe it does. Rather, it comes from their need to feel secure, to know whom they are dealing with and the parameters of the situation.

Eights admire strength and honesty in others. They can be very vindictive if they feel injured, especially if the hurt is done unfairly. Eights will use revenge as an emotional buffer in order to feel strong and to punish those who have threatened them. They can also be especially vindictive if someone gets too close to their wounded "marshmallow" inner self. Eights are usually not aware of this fragile inner part.

If Eights feel overwhelmed and do not lash out, they might withdraw to an "inner fortress" in order to survive in what they perceive as a frightening world.

Eights can be utterly amoral. They can verify guidelines and then see themselves as bigger than the rules, taking whatever it is that they want. They love to follow their impulses and desires. For Eights it is essential to get more of what feels good. This can be extremes and excesses, overstimulation, danger, living on the edge of life's experiences to reinforce being alive.

Denial is key for understanding Eights. They operate in such a way that they can easily remain inattentive to their own weakness and vulnerability.

How Being an Eight Can Affect Personal Behavior

Eights lust for excess. This can create problems for them. Their need for too much, too soon, too loud, for too long, can lead to their pushing their minds, bodies, and emotions to collapse.

Denial of their own fear, their own weakness, their need for others, and their vulnerability can harm Eights and force them into painful periods of isolation and loss of what is important to them. This can be work, relationships, or enjoyable opportunities. Eights have a self-defeating need to have control and tendency toward domination that may get counterattacked by others. Eights may then experience unnecessary loss and defeat of their goals. This may also occur if Eights experience conflicts with authority over their control issues.

Eights can confuse what they view as justice with their own self-referenced desire for revenge. When they do this, they delude themselves as well as hurt others.

Eights find it difficult to expose their deepest wishes and to initiate real goals. They fear rejection and hurt and do not feel skilled in sticking up for their own fragile, deeply personal needs. By keeping the wall up, Eights can miss out on the blessings that can come to them. They miss out on the life experiences of receiving tenderness, of being free to admit their weaknesses, and of experiencing the power of others' compassion for them and the power of the practice of compassion with others.

How the Eight Is Perceived by Others

Others can feel driven away by the Eights' excesses and need for control. They can resent Eights' stance of intimidation and intrusiveness.

When Eights violate the rights of others, or do them harm, either bodily or emotionally, those violated may feel anger and hurt. They may feel violated and belittled when continued patterns of vulgarity, aggression, or insensitivity persist. They will eventually find a way to remove the Eight from their lives.

If Eights become bored, they tend to interfere or meddle in affairs that are not their areas of responsibility. Others may resent this.

Security and Stress Points: Two and Five

If you have not yet determined if you are using the Eight as a habit of mind, look at the arrows in the graph of the Enneagram in Figure 13. Perhaps you will recognize more about yourself by seeing if you have "spent time" in your life at Point Two or Five.

Security Point: Two

This is where, when happy, when drawing upon the strengths of Eights' own Point, they observe themselves living with the higher aspects of Point Two. When Eights experience themselves as more secure, as stronger in themselves, they have the psychic strength to swim against the flow of the arrow, to grow and reach to the higher aspects of the Two. This also enhances their lives as they experience living with higher aspects of their own point.

Eights operating out of their higher qualities find that they can relate comfortably with others. They can be very helpful, compassionate, and generous. They become able to simplify their lives, being more childlike, able to admit that they have weaknesses and needs. They become able to embrace their own "tender inner marshmallow."

There does remain in discussion, too, the theory that when experiencing personal stress, individuals also draw upon the lower aspects of the Security Point as a resource. If you think you might be an Eight, look at the higher and lower aspects of Point Two.

Stress Point: Five

To see the Eights' Stress Point, follow the arrow to Point Five. This is where, when experiencing what Eights perceive as excessive pressure, they draw upon the lower aspects of Point Five. They coast, so to speak, along the arrow to another, safer, more protective space.

Eights who are in stress and are in this space feel inferior and "no good." Their strategy is to withdraw from others, to brood, to be as unapproachable as a fully sealed "Tiger Tank." Eights in this space can also act with destructive hostility.

Again, I would remind the reader that there does remain in discussion the theory that when individuals experience security, they can draw also upon the higher aspects of their Stress Point Read the higher aspects of this Point to understand Eights a little better.

PART 2

The Side Points (Wings): Seven and Nine

In considering the influence of the sides of your Point, read the entire descriptions of the two sides, Point Seven and Point Nine. Observe yourself and your patterns honestly. If you have patterns that run you, this is something to let go of. If you have patterns that you use in a healthy, wholesome way, then own this too.

The Basic Instincts (Subtypes)

One-on-one Instinct/Subtype: Possession, Surrender

Eights in the one-on-one subtype need to know as much as possible about their significant other. They like intensity in their relationships. They need to know the inner mind, heart, and soul of the other. They feel secure and can reduce their defenses when they know as much as possible about the other.

The surrender aspect of this subtype is seen when Eights trust their significant other without reservation. Eights can trust to such an extent that they feel free to give up their obsessive need to control their partner.

Social Instinct/Subtype: Friendship

Eights in this subtype are very friendly. They extend the gift of friendship to those they trust. They extend this to those they protect who are weaker than themselves and to those they see as protecting them.

Self-preservation Instinct/Subtype: Satisfactory Survival

Eights in this subtype focus on the control of details necessary for their personal survival and space. Their preoccupation with their survival needs replaces any other level of concern for their other areas of personal needs.

When the Eight Can Finally Surrender

Eights may open up more easily to change if their significant other (family, friends) express profound concern for them and their behaviors.

They might realize a need to "let God in" if they experience the following more than they want to: interventions by the courts; problems with valued coworkers; repeated or extended periods of depression; consequences caused by excessive substance abuse, whether food, alcohol, or drugs.

ABOUT THE NINE

FIGURE 14

POINT NINE

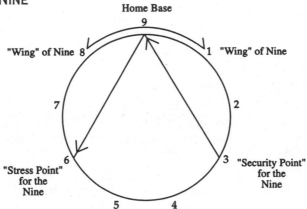

The name the Nine is called:
   Mediator (Palmer)
   Peacemaker (Riso)
   Need to Avoid (Rohr)
   Going With the Stream (Naranjo)
   Negotiator (Beesing, Nogosek, and O'Leary)

What grabs the Nine's attention:
   Feeling calm and content, others' positions

What the Nine avoids:
   Conflict

The Nine's trait, obsession, defect:
   Sloth, laziness

How the Nine Pays Attention

The focus of Nines is to pay attention to other people's positions, to sense their wishes. Nines find it more comfortable to do as others wish, or to find a common ground between differing parties. They do well at seeing the position of others, but they have difficulty with knowing their own positions.

Their anger shows as stubbornness. They can leave conflicts mentally by tuning out others, "pushing the vulnerability button" of others, tripping them into anger. When Nines do feel anger, they tend to contain it within themselves.

The sloth of Nines is a spiritual lack where they are lazy about remembering themselves. Palmer describes this as a type of "self-forgetting." Nines do things that drain their energy and attention away from their own goals and interests. They appear lazy because they pay attention to nonessentials that divert their energies from their priorities. They "self-forget" by becoming preoccupied with small comforts and substitutes for love.

Nines surrender their attention to addictive habits so that life can become more automatic for them. Some of their addictive habits include craving drugs, food, alcohol, and "numbing out" on television and gossip.

Nines can find themselves stuck in inertia and depression or bound in jealousy of others whom they cannot move. They experience what is referred to by Palmer as "armchair depression."

When in conversation, Nines exhibit a capacity for receiving many details at the same time. This is like a "coprocessing" mind because all details are received with equal status. They can also receive from several conversations at the same time, e.g., listening to television and talking with someone.

Nines like their own familiar situations and routine. They like to design their own structure so that they can act through the comfort of automatic habits.

Nines frequently accumulate things. This capacity of Nines gives whole new meaning to the word *clutter*. They do this by taking on more without letting go of any of their things. They feel they "might need something of it" someday. This accumulation is not only seen in things but also unfinished business, memories, information, symbols, and hobbies.

How Being a Nine Can Affect Personal Behavior

Nines can become very angry with themselves for taking on the positions of others instead of their own. They can shove this anger down, denying it. Their denial can result in psychosomatic illnesses such as high blood pressure, arthritis, obesity, or depression. When

Nines do show their anger, this can be as a passivity that holds them back from doing what they might really want to do.

Nines can feel very lost because of their pattern of forgetting themselves, their interests, and their goals. Because of this habit of self-sedation through whatever means, Nines can feel even more lost because they don't know what is important to them.

Nines' habit of doing what makes them comfortable can lead to great frustration for them. They develop an inertia and become unable to do what is important to them.

As with anger, when Nines contain their energy for so long, they find they don't have it to use when they want to do so.

Nines can also experience extreme suffering and disappointment with themselves when they miss opportunities through their delays in making decisions or being "unfocused."

How the Nine Is Perceived by Others

Nines' habits of passive aggression, of being stubborn and "numbing out," can chase others away from interactions with them.

Nines can miss the point of what is really important to those in the group. This can frustrate others.

Nines can miss recognizing real needs in others. They give generously what they want to give, but this might not be what the other feels is needed. On the other hand, others may experience frustration because they might not be clear as to what to give to the Nine.

Nines can appear to agree with others in a conversation. This may not be the case, as Nines often are not mentally present for conversations. Others can become very angry at this.

Nines' pattern of dominating others by remaining in comfortable patterns can frustrate others, especially if the others seek routines not chosen by Nines or if they wish to have more spontaneity.

Nines merge with others. They can frequently describe others' feelings better than their own. This can be difficult for those in relationships with Nines because when others wish to love Nines, they "can't find them." A question asked of Nines can be, "Where are you?" (Palmer).

Nines want to be consulted, but they like to have their opinions drawn out by others. Others can resent being required to do this.

Nines' need to maintain their world their way can lead to a type of autonomy that may leave others feeling left out.

Security and Stress Points: Three and Six

If you have not yet determined if you are using the Nine as a habit of mind, look at the graph of the Enneagram in Figure 14. Look at the arrows, and see if any aspects of those numbers reflect how you have lived.

Security Point: Three

This is where, when happy, when drawing upon the strengths of the Nines' own Point, they observe themselves living with the higher aspects of Point Three. When Nines experience themselves as more secure, as stronger "inside their own skin," they have the psychic strength to swim against the flow of the arrow, to grow and reach to the higher aspects of the Three. This also enhances their lives as they experience living with higher aspects of their own Point.

When Nines feels secure and are developing their own higher aspects, they can claim their own thoughts, positions, and projects. They find the energy to act. They come to life, letting themselves be competent. They notice that they have developed skills within themselves. They know how to resolve conflicts constructively.

There does remain in discussion, too, the theory that when experiencing personal stress, individuals also draw upon the lower aspects of the Security Point as a resource. If you think you might be a Nine, look at the higher and lower aspects of Point Three.

Stress Point: Six

To see Nines' Stress Point, follow the arrow to Point Six. This is where, when experiencing what Nines perceive as excessive pressure, they draw upon the lower aspects of Point Six. They coast, so to speak, along the arrow to another, safer, more protective space.

Nines can doubt their own authority when they are under stress. When drawing upon the lower aspects of the Six, they can become indecisive and suspicious of others. They can become overdependent on the rules, the laws of the environment to which they want to belong.

Again, I would remind the reader that there does remain in discussion the theory that when individuals experience security, they also can draw upon the higher aspects of their Stress Point. Read the higher aspects of this Point to understand Nines a little better.

The Side Points (Wings): Eight and One

In considering the influence of the sides of your Point, read the entire descriptions of the two sides, Point One and Point Eight. Observe yourself and your patterns honestly. If you have patterns that run you, this is something to let go of. If you have patterns that you use in a healthy, wholesome way, then own this too.

The Basic Instincts (Subtypes)

One-on-one Instinct/Subtype: Seeking Union

Nines in the sexual subtype desire to merge completely with their significant other. They seek a type of communion of being "at one" with the other.

There is frequently another pattern in Nines in this subtype. They can also seek a personal union with their inner source of being, the Divine. This can consume Nines as a drive that satisfies, protects, and can also hold them back from engaging in reality especially when done to the point of excess and imbalance.

Social Instinct/Subtype: Participation

The social subtype is usually of two types. Nines can have a total aversion to joining groups, living independently of others as much as possible. This reduces the demands upon them to decide and act. Other Nines might like to relax and be around a special-activity club or a group of friends. These Nines are attracted to the energy of people doing something together. This serves Nines as a pleasant distraction, while they can feel free to dip in and out of the energy flowing around them.

Self-preservation Instinct/Subtype: Appetite

Nines in this subtype replace their essential wishes with inessential substitutes such as too much food, TV, novels, hobby interests. They can also engage in projects such as collecting voluminous amounts of information about secondary pursuits. These substitute for deep hungers of which they are not yet aware.

When the Nine Can Finally Surrender

When Nines get into contact with their childhood patterns, they often become ready to accept help. As children, Nines discounted their own essential needs. They might have been neglected, ignored, or over-shadowed by their siblings. They might have been attacked for standing up for their own ideas. They might have learned that showing anger did not help their position to be heard. They also may have learned that if they waited around long enough, they could get what they wanted in the first place.

When Nines see the extent that they are still working out of the past as if it is now, they become free to let go of it, especially if these strategies have more adverse consequences than they are ready to encounter.

Nines become ready to surrender if they have been misusing food, alcohol, drugs, and as a consequence of their inertia, their lives are becoming more unmanageable than they are willing to live with.

If Nines lose something or someone they really value as a result of their behavior, they can become ready to change.

When they find their rage surfacing, and if this scares them, Nines can become very uncomfortable. If the feedback from others is also extensive, these two influences can help Nines become ready to surrender.

How to Begin to Walk Step One

Now that you have observed yourself a little, you have noticed patterns seducing you with their allure. You have begun to see how powerful their influence is in your life. You are ready to take Step One. Your question is, "How do I do this?"

The whole point of this Step is to admit that you are powerless. For each of you, regardless of your Point, this is really hard to do. It hurts, and you resist it. When you are ready to practice these Twelve Steps, and to take Step One, you will know it. For now it is enough to stay at this Step. Give yourself permission to slow down and just "be." Be open to observe yourself. When you work, rest, and eat, let yourself be aware and see what grabs your attention. If it is food, as you put it into your mouth when you don't want to, remember this moment. When you are ready, you'll feel yourself getting angry, sad, fearful, or frustrated, and you'll finally get ready to say, "Enough, I give up!" Congratulations— you will have done the hardest part of the spiritual journey. Nothing else will be needed for right now. That's it. You will have done Step One.

If you are not yet ready to take Step One, but you want to be, here are some possible activities to find help to take Step One. Meanwhile, be kind to yourself. You are trying, and this is good.

1. Notice the History of Your Behavior

You've read the Enneagram Points summary. What did you see in yourself? What came to your mind? Stay with this for a bit. For some people it is helpful to talk this out with another person. In Part 5, I will say more about picking a special person with whom you can share your journey.

You might want to sit down for a few moments each day to do this "remembering." You could go away for a day or two to think and to remember without distractions around you. There are some individuals who have felt it helpful to keep on with their routines but to allow the thoughts and feelings to come and go, observing them carefully.

Let yourself muse. What experiences about your childhood come to you? How did you feel? Write down some of these thoughts, feelings, memories. Memories can be as recent as your current patterns, feelings, relationships. They do not have to be from childhood. Sometimes more is revealed to you as you continue the journey. It is not necessary to have full enlightenment at the beginning of a journey.

2. Observe Yourself

A proven strategy to help you grow is to be still and listen. Try it. Try sitting or lying comfortably so that your back is straight. Let yourself breathe in deeply through your nose. Let the air out through your nose or mouth. Anthony[5] suggests you imagine that you "Breathe in...Security. Breathe out...Calm." Do this slowly for a few minutes, up to twenty minutes at first. Perhaps some thoughts or feelings might come to mind. Let them in with respect, then gently let go of them. They will come later for you to remember and to see in yourself.

A really wonderful way to do this self-observation is to join with a few others. Put on a relaxing, quiet musical tape. Practice the breathing. Be still along with the others in the room. Write down whatever comes to your mind. Just write. Do nothing else for now.

3. Thoughts to Trigger Memories, Self-awareness

Below are some thoughts that might help you trigger memories or self-awareness. Pick some pattern you read in the list below. Write about it. Include answers to reflection questions such as: How do you feel about yourself? Has it always been this way? Do you want to let go of this pattern, or is it fine with you? The real spiritual journey needs every part of you—the head, the heart, and the gut instincts— so keep on doing this. You *will* be led to deeper memories and self-awareness.

Thoughts about my patterns:

I have difficulty having fun.
I have difficulty doing anything that is not fun.
I take myself very, very seriously.
I don't take myself seriously at all.
I am superresponsible.
I am superirresponsible.
I am extremely loyal even if the person doesn't deserve it.
I tend to lock myself into a course of action.
I have difficulty with intimacy in relationships.
I judge others without mercy.
I lie when it is easy to tell the truth.

I have trouble following a project through to the end.
I have to guess at what normal is. The experience eludes me.
I overreact to stress and to changes I control.
I often seek approval or affirmation.
I feel different from other people.

4. Select Someone to Share With

Many religious traditions and cultures in the East and West have a long-standing precedent of using a spiritual companion. More of this is discussed in Part 5, so I will not say too much here.

As you share your deepest self, as you open yourself to another, you come to see that in some way, deep within yourself, you do have a need for God or something or someone outside yourself. In some way your life is not really manageable by yourself. You need a new habit, a new way of responding, a happier, more honest, more relational, more secure life inside your own skin or with others or maybe with your God.

5. Give the Scriptures a Try

In Appendices 4 and 5 in Part 6, I have organized a summary of possible Scripture verses to serve as resources for reflection. They are offered for all the higher and lower aspects of the Enneagram, and each of the Twelve Steps.

Read these verses. Let your mind, heart, and gut instincts receive whatever comes. This can be powerful and very enlightening. It can be a way to find your Enneagram Point, or to receive support in taking each Enneagram Step.

First Step Prayer

When you are ready to take Step One, some expression can be helpful for you to help yourself know you are really ready. This expression can also be through tears of frustration, a desperate groan, a prayer.

A suggested prayer might be the following, but feel free to write your own or just pray spontaneously:

Today I am asking for help with my compulsions and character weaknesses. Denial has kept me from seeing how powerless and stuck I really am. My life is not manageable! I need to learn and remember that I have developed patterns that I need to change. Help me! Please, help me!

When you believe you have taken Step One, Step Two is ready and waiting for you.

Chapter 4

Step Two: Begin to Really Believe

Step Two: "Came to believe that a Power greater than ourselves could restore us to sanity."

Sanity means wholeness. It means balance. Once you have clearly taken Step One, you know very well that you have a real need to change. Your challenge is to allow yourself to "come to," to "wake up." It's as if you have been in a slumber, a state of self-delusion, and you want to take off the blinders. You want a new, better prescription for your new eyes.

There are only possibilities to assent to at this Step. The first is to come to the place in your heart where you can let yourself allow for the possibility that you are not the center of the universe. The second thing to assent to is that there is some force, something bigger than you, in your life. This may be love, it may be your compulsion, it may be a group of people, it may be God. You assent to something greater than yourself in your life.

You might say, "What does this have to do with getting over a fixation?" Unless you can open up to the possibility of something bigger than yourself being a reality, you can never open up to being on the receiving end of anyone or anything. The real invitation in this journey of the Twelve Steps and the Enneagram is the invitation to believe you are lovable and you are loved. You come to believe you can let go of how you have been. You can become powerfully renewed. Ephesians 4:22-24 is one of many texts that come to mind at this Step:

You were taught to put away your former way of life, your old self, corrupt and deluded by its lusts, and to be renewed in the spirit of your minds and to clothe yourselves with the new self, created according to the likeness of God in true righteousness and holiness.

In this Step you show up for the journey. You agree to come. You "come to" with a new awareness of your need. Gradually, with openness and through listening to your heart, you are finally ready to "come to believe."

At this Step, even if it feels foolish, you accept the possibility that you can become a happy, loving, powerful, positive, creative person. You accept the possibility that some Higher Power, or God, can guide you to wholeness.

In this Step you continue the work of observing yourself and how you have lived. You continue to watch yourself as you do the work of taking and retaking Step One. You share with your special companion. (See Part 5.) As you do this, the dawning comes slowly but surely that you are already being helped to see new possibilities. With this insight comes a new belief that a power greater than yourself is helping you.

Some people have problems with this Step because the Twelve Steps don't specifically give the Higher Power a name such as Jesus, Yahweh, Lord. This is for a reason. At this Step there is no denial of any one of the many names for God, but the reality is that this is a spiritual journey, not a religious one. Religion helps you to develop teachings about God and gives you names for God, but every religion builds upon each person's own solid, spiritual foundation.

As you work these Steps, you will see that your religious path will emerge or deepen as this spiritual journey progresses. It will be all the more real for practicing your own work freely and personally.

The reality is also that individuals baptized into particular religious groups or churches have always followed the tenets of their church. This is good, but deep down in their own lives they must also go deeply to develop their own real personal relationship with their God, a mature interdependence with their God. The dependency they have developed is upon the personality patterns and their fixations and habits that have worked for them up until now. It is necessary to let people come to their own individual "reassent" to the name they choose for their Higher Power.

Step Two is a beginning that allows for something greater than yourself to exist in your life. Step Two allows you to open up to the possibility that you will be restored to being an even better person. This is good and very important.

Individuals need to grow at their own pace. The Twelve Steps have helped many people experience profound and lasting transformation. At this Step you get to honor this need. You look at your own need. You're stuck. You said so in Step One. Now you look at yourself and your needs. You don't take the time now for theological disputes or criticism or analysis of this Step. You open up to trust that your own Higher Power will help you and restore you as needed.

Some Strategies to Work Step Two

Below you will find some helpful strategies for taking Step Two. These have been shared with me in my own spiritual growth and throughout my research for this book.

1. Use Your Companion

Let go of any "oughts," and share honestly what is going on within you. Let yourself feel and "be with yourself" as you experience many "ups and downs." When you open up to letting go of how you have become, you are risking a lot. This is threatening and scary. All individuals want to control. This is a human need. To open up to new possibilities is very hard. Don't put guilt trips on yourself that you "should have had more faith in God already," especially if you are a religious person. Just be, and share yourself as you are.

2. Write a Letter to Your Old God

Write your insights, fears, joys, ideas, as you walk this Step. Write your letter as an ongoing daily diary for a while, if this is helpful. Share the letter with someone, if you want, then *burn* it! "Let go" of it as part of the universe, now. After you have written it, shared it, and burned it, let yourself have some special time to be very still and grieve this loss. Change can be very hard. Even new insights can be difficult. It is very important to respect this and to allow your healing process to happen.

3. Write a Letter to Your New God

Write a letter to your new God about how you feel. Express your hopes, your insecurity, your wishes. Share your letter with someone. Let yourself feel your feelings. Save this letter.

4. Express Your New Belief With Some Ritual

After you have walked through this Step, use some gesture or ritual to express your awareness that you "have come to believe that a Power greater than yourself can restore you to sanity."

One way to do this is to stand and hold up your hands in some movement of openness or humility. Try it, and you will find a position that is comfortable.

Another way to do this is to write your own prayer to your new God. Read it out loud.

Another way is to pray the Second Step prayer below.

Second Step Prayer

I thank you for letting me come to believe in some Power greater than myself. I pray for the humility and openness to let this real belief continue to grow deeply inside me.

When you have come to know that you are not alone, that you do have a Higher Power, it is time to do the groundwork necessary to make the decision of Step Three.

Chapter 5

Step Three: Turn It Over

Step Three: "Made a decision to turn our will and our lives over to the care of God as we understood Him."

Step Three leads you to accept God's power in your life. In Step Two you have come to the openness to want the revolution to happen. You might have come to believe that change could really happen. So far you have opened up to the possibility that you have a need (Step One) and that God could help you if you will seek for help (Step Two).

In Step Three you make a specific commitment to "let go and let God" take over in your life. You open up to a spiritual revolution. Picture yourself walking down a street, making a 180-degree turn, and walking in the opposite direction. This is a complete change in direction, a revolution.

In Step Three you make a decision to "let go" and to let the revolution begin. You do not decide this only in your head, but you profess a dedication to this decision. It is important to remember that you don't decide to change. You are not in charge. Rather, you decide to "turn your will and your life over to the care of God as you understand Him." You give consent in Step Three to let God be God and to surrender the job to him.

Up until now you have let yourself be deluded that your habits, your patterns, were *good* for you when in fact, they were *God* for you. Now you are speaking of trusting a new God, or at least a God who is newly met again.

When you speak of this trust, it is helpful if you use your own words. It is good to let yourself develop your own sense of who you are at this time and who God is for you. There seems to be a need for time with this Step, especially for those of you who were raised in church traditions that are heavily based upon teachings of sin and guilt. Sometimes individuals raised in strong church traditions haven't really found God in their own hearts. Rather, they have accepted theological teachings but have not yet deepened to allow the Spirit to touch their hearts with trust and confidence. This is a sensitive matter.

Please understand that no criticism is meant of any church or religion that presents specific teachings of faith and morals. Rather, the problem can be in how an individual has internalized these teachings. The Twelve Steps are a resource for developing a spiritual life. Right now, you are concentrating on your own personal relationship with a God and yourself, nothing else. The rest will follow if you but take these Steps carefully and seriously.

The following is a reflection perfect for this Third Step preparation, so I include it here.[6]

YOUR GOD

I am your God...and I am close to you...and whether you realize it or not, that is enough. What more could you want or need? My love is ready to fill your life....

I am your God...and I am faithful to you...even when sorrows come. Remember, I am still with you. I am. I am still. I am with you.

I am your God...and I think of you...from all eternity I have been thinking about you....I have written your name in my heart...I will never, never forget you.

I am your God...and I am arranging everything for your happiness....You may not understand it all now...Do not worry...One day you will understand everything...I will explain it to you.

I am your God...and I love you so much...I know all that makes you sad, I see those things that make you wince with pain....Accept everything with tranquility and great peace...because I know what is happening. For reasons that you do not understand now, I will allow many things that cause you pain....Do not worry about this, be faithful to me, for you are part of the plan I have...and I count on you....My love will be your strength.

I am your God...do you feel all alone? I am here....You feel that no one speaks to you or understands? Come close to me...I will be to you a compensation for everything else....

I am your God....What more could you want or need? Once you let me BE your God, you will know such peace and joy that nothing could ever be too hard....Do not worry about anything. My love is all you need....Take it!!!!

The world is passing away....Time is passing away....Death will take you from everything you now know....Do not worry, for I will be there. I wait for you...and it is my deepest joy to be...

Your God

Some Activities to Help You Take Step Three

1. Write a Letter (or a Poem) to God
Describe what making a decision to turn your will and your life over to some Higher Power means to you. You could include how many times you've tried to change your thoughts, your feelings, your behaviors. Write your feelings, frustrations, delights, successes, ambivalence. Include why you think you haven't been able to change yet.

2. Write a Letter to Yourself
This sounds weird to do, but it can be done in the imagination, if you put your pen to the paper and try it.
Write a letter to your body. Include what you have done to it so far and what you think you would like to do differently.
Write a letter to your mind. List what you have done to it so far and what you think you would like to do differently.

Write a letter to your emotions. List how you have treated them so far. Include how you have listened to them and how you have ignored them. Write what you would like to do differently, to have a different relationship with yourself.

Write a letter to yourself about how you have engaged in work. List what you have done so far and how you would like to act differently.

Write a letter to yourself about how you have engaged in play. Include how you have abused the privileges of play and recreation. Include how you have restricted yourself from being able to engage in enough play and leisure. Write what you would like to do differently.

Write a letter to yourself about how you have lived spiritually. Include how you have prayed and not prayed. Include how you have tried to operate without a real dependence on God and how you have let God be a partner in your life so far. Write what you would like to do differently.

Write a letter to yourself about your relationships. Include what they have been like. Include what you would like to do differently.

After writing the letters, share them with someone. Then let go of this by tearing them up and burning them. Later on, if there is more writing to do, you will remember easily what you need to remember.

3. Make a Commitment Out Loud

The important thing is to take this Step very seriously as a commitment. Do it with your companion or a special friend. When you do this with another person, you no longer do this in secret all alone. There is no room on this trip for those who choose to isolate or do it by themselves. It just does not seem as effective! You should not do this alone because this is not a Step for making decisions as if you are in control. Rather, it is a Step to relax and observe yourself even more than before. It is a step to observe how you have let yourself become and to allow for possibilities to change you. You agree to let go of the illusion of being in control, or out of control, and to "turn it over" to this higher, better, and deeper Power within your being.

To express your commitment, you can write your own prayer or use the one suggested below.

Third Step Prayer

God, I offer myself to you, to build with me and to do with me as you will. Relieve me of the bondage of my self that I may better do your will. Take away my difficulties so that victory over them may bear witness to those I would help of your power in my life, your love, your way of life. Amen.[7]

Section Three begins with a reflection upon the next Step on the journey, Step Four.

Notes

[1] In the AA literature this Step reads: "We admitted we were powerless over alcohol, and that our lives had become unmanageable." Since many do not struggle with alcohol or its effects upon others, this Step actually reads: "powerless over life and life's conditions." The readers are welcome to substitute any reality that is more helpful for them in their growth.

[2] Matthew 5:3. This is a core teaching of Christ, yet it is often minimized by those who view themselves as his disciples.

[3] Ephesians 4:22–24.

[4] Matthew 7:3–5 and Luke 6:41–42.

[5] Anthony, Edd. *Reflections on the Serenity Prayer*, Audiotape (Victorville: Franciscan Canticle, Inc., 1992).

[6] Susan Cogan, "Your God," *Intercom*. International of the English Province of the Daughters of Mary and Joseph. 55 Fitzjames Avenue, Croydon, Surrey CRO 5DN.

[7] This prayer is paraphrased from the AA reference, *Alcoholics Anonymous*, Chapter Five, page 63.

PART 3

Steps Four Through Eleven

Chapter 6

Step Four: Take a Good Look at Yourself!

Step Four: "Made a searching and fearless moral inventory of ourselves."

When this Step is described in the AA literature, it is stressed that this is a *moral* inventory. It is not an inventory of immoral or wrong actions only. It is a time for you to look at your life honestly. As described in the book *Alcoholics Anonymous,* "No business lasts for long without regularly taking stock of their inventory. When the stock taking is done, one writes what assets and materials are in stock, and what has been spent, used or lost."[1]

In Step Four you take an honest look at your life, your gifts, your assets, your strengths, as well as your weaknesses, deficits, obsessions, defects, and sins. You may write about negative events such as anger, resentment, fear, harms, and hurts, but you are not necessarily writing about sin. Some of what you write *may* be about sin as taught by specific churches. In this inventory, however, you are trying to take an honest look at your life. What you attempt here is to observe how you have been operating. You are seeking self-knowledge, not self-judgment.

The AA literature gives much attention to the topic of how you operate out of your instincts. David Daniels, a psychiatrist working with the Enneagram, describes the development of your instinctual patterns as your "habits of attention." He describes their development as the result of what you experienced when operating at a more instinctual level. A summary of his reflection would be as follows.[2]

You begin with your three basic subtypes of self-preservation, sexual (one-on-one), and social (small group). As you grow and begin to perceive threats, you experience anxiety, which creates in turn a type of preoccupation for you. From this preoccupation you attempt different ways of responding to others and your environment. Eventually, you settle upon a pattern that works for you. You use it repetitively. As you use it repetitively, it becomes a habit. This is called a "habit of attention." With the Enneagram you are looking at your life to see the extent you need to let go of your patterns more specifically.

Part of the inventory in Step Four is to claim with honesty the gifts, the assets of the Point that you feel you typify. These are good. You need them in your life, for yourself, for your relationships with others, and in relationship with your God.

Part of what you also need to claim are those aspects of your habits that have come to control you. They have taken over to interrupt your personal life, your relationships with others, and, your relationship with God. In the rest of these Steps you will see how to turn around this aspect of your pattern. You will remain who you are essentially, but you will find yourself freed to foster the higher aspects of your life, the gifts, in a way far beyond your wildest expectations.

In taking this Step, you accept the invitation to look at your life as the beginning of a lifetime practice of self-observation. You look in a searching way at your fears, at your resentments, at the harms and hurts you have done, and at the harms and hurts that have been done to you. You name the instincts that have been threatened and your responses to them. You come to see what has developed into character defects as well as what has developed into character assets. You come to see specifically how you have been growing and how you have yet to grow.

In Step Four the word *fearless* is very important. If you find yourself resisting this inventory because you are scared to do it, perhaps you need to wait. You might need to allow for more deepening in Steps One, Two, and Three. Perhaps there is a need to take this journey a little more slowly. *Alcoholics Anonymous* suggests that an individual begin immediately with Step Four after Step Three, but you have to have taken Step Three well, first.[3]

When you know that you are powerless, sick, and tired of what you have become (Step One), when you have come to believe that you can be helped to be fully whole again (Step Two); and when you have been able to make that decision to turn your will and your life over to the care of God as you understand him (Step Three), then, and only then, are you ready to take this Step Four fearlessly. The time will come—just be patient with yourself. Be honest and patient with those who you assist with these Steps as well.

If you feel you are ready and you have discussed this with your special companion, it is time to begin Step Four. You are ready to prepare a fearless and "searching" moral inventory. I have listed some ways to prepare this inventory, but please remember that these are only suggestions. With your Higher Power, and the help of your companion, you will find the method that is best for you.

Some Ways to Take Your Inventory

1. Write a Reflection on Your Anger, Resentments, Fears, Harms, and Hurts

The book *Alcoholics Anonymous* suggests a method that I will summarize here. Even though anger, resentments, fears, harms, and hurts are more accessible to some persons and Enneagram Points than they are to others, they are realities known to each one of you.

When you begin to write your Fourth Step, you may find you do not have much to say about one area or another. This is all right. For example, the first time I wrote an inventory, I had twenty pages on "anger," "resentment," and "fear," but half a page on "harms and hurts." Later, five years later, I wrote another Fourth Step. I wrote twenty-six pages on the "harms and hurts" I had done to others and that had been done to me. Be patient with yourself. As the literature suggests, "more will be revealed."

There are many ways to do this reflection. One of these is offered here. In this approach, each page would focus on the same one emotion. Make several columns on a paper. Draw lines down the page to divide the page as shown in Figure 15.

FIGURE 15

INVENTORY LIST

TIMES I HAVE BEEN ANGRY/RESENTFUL			
COLUMN 1	COLUMN 2	COLUMN 3	COLUMN 4
Situation, Cause People, Event Principals, Institution	What Happened Specifics Why Was I: Angry? Resentful?	What Part of Myself Was Affected Social, Security, Sexual Instincts, Subtypes	Result: My Wrongs Mistakes Faults

When I speak of anger and resentment, I refer to feelings of bitter hurt or indignation that come from feelings, rightly or wrongly held, of being injured or offended.

In column 1 write what comes to mind when you think of being angry or resentful. Some person may come to mind. Write the person's name. Perhaps other things may come to mind. Jot down the situation you were in, a conversation, something that happened in a particular place, or even principles you were required to live under or to live with.

Some people might say, "Well I'm in the *fear* center, so I do not need to do this." This is possible, but I suggest that you at least give it a try. You never know what might surface if you let your Higher Power help you.

In column 2 write the specifics that made you angry and how you responded to them. Write your part of the situation or interaction, if this applies.

In column 3 write which basic instinct (subtype) was affected. All of these instincts are important to have for a normal, healthy life. It is important to look at the extent to which you live out each of the subtypes. There might be a pattern that will be helpful for you to see. You may learn the extent to which there is an imbalance in how you operate.

Some examples of how your instincts or subtypes can be affected are offered here as possibilities.

Figure 16 offers a summary of column 3 for reference.

FIGURE 16

INSTINCTS/SUBTYPES AFFECTED (COLUMN THREE)

SELF-PRESERVATION	SEXUAL (ONE ON ONE)	SOCIAL
Material	Acceptable Sex	Companionship
Emotional	Hidden	Prestige, Self-esteem
Ambitions	Ambitions	Pride, Personal
		Relationships
		Ambitions

If any area has been threatened or thwarted, one can experience anger, resentment, fear, hurt, or harm.

It is very important to honor this by writing in the third column.

Below is a summary of the three instinct areas. These are listed in Figure 16.

Self-preservation Instinct

Material. This includes your "wants" for money, buildings, investments, property, clothing, in order to be safe and secure in the future.

Emotional. Your needs for feeling secure by being in positions, situations, relationships, where you either dominate others or are overly dependent upon them.

Ambitions. Your plans to have material things, wealth, clothes, property, success, jobs, so that you can be in a dominant position or so that you manipulate others to depend upon you.

Sexual (One-on-One) Instinct

Acceptable Sex. As a human being , you are either male or female. Given the human drive for companionship, you might belong to groups with certain expectations or determinations of acceptable sexual behavior, including one-on-one relationships, which you hold as important for you. Some of you might be married, some single, some holding certain principles as from God. You all hold some personal values that have been formed according to your own principles. The important issue is to try to be honest in determining if it is acceptable sexual instinct and one-on-one relationships that have been affected.

Hidden. In this area you look at your sexual life, your one-on-one relationships that are contrary to either society, God's principles as you believe them to be, or your own principles. Are you angry or resentful because you have been thwarted? Are you fearful because of how you have been treated or how you have acted? Have you done harms or hurts to others in this area, or had them done to you? If so, this area has been affected.

Ambitions. This area is about your plans for sexuality or one-on-one relationships in an area that is either acceptable or hidden. If thwarted, this can lead to anger, resentment, fears, harms or hurts to yourself or others. If so, this area has been affected.

Social Instinct

Companionship. You need to belong and to be accepted, and you might perceive this as being threatened.

Prestige. You want to be recognized as a leader. You want a significant, (what you consider to be) respectable place within the group.

Self-esteem. This is how you think of yourself, how you feel about yourself, whether as high self-esteem or low self-esteem.

Pride. Though there is a healthy self-love as self-esteem, pride refers to an excessive and unjustified opinion of yourself, either as a positive, "better than others" self-love, or as a negative, "lesser than others" self-hate.

Personal Relationships. This refers to your relations with other people and patterns you bring to the groups around you.

Ambitions. This refers to your plans for achieving acceptance, power, recognition, prestige, and so forth.

In column 4 write your part in the event you remembered. Write your response if you were selfish, dishonest, self-seeking, frightened, or inconsiderate.

After writing about the area of anger and resentments, begin writing about the area of fears. Figure 17 presents a sample of one way to do this writing.

FIGURE 17

TIMES I HAVE BEEN AFRAID

COLUMN 1	COLUMN 2	COLUMN 3	COLUMN 4
Situation, Cause People, Event Prinipals, Institution	What Happened Specifics Why Was I: Angry? Resentful? Afraid?	What Part of Myself Was Affected? Social, Security, Sexual Instincts, Subtypes	Result: My Wrongs Mistakes Faults

When I refer to feelings of fear, I mean any feelings of anxiety, agitation, uneasiness, or apprehension you may have experienced.

In order to make it easier for you to understand this way of writing, I include a sample of what you might want to write as Figure 18.

FIGURE 18

SAMPLE WRITING ON FEAR

TIMES I HAVE BEEN AFRAID			
Cause?	Why?	Part of Me	My Wrongs
Susan	She expected me to do the project, and I knew I couldn't.	My need to control. My need to be listened to.	I refused to meet her deadline; she lost the accoount.
My employer	Disapproval of my work when he asked me to do it.	Need, ambition for financial security, self-esteem, and survival needs.	Blamed someone else. Lied to him. Lied to myself.

After writing in the area of fears, begin with the area of harms and hurts. When I refer to harms and hurts, I mean those wrong acts that result in pain, hurt feelings, worry, financial loss, for others as well as yourself.

A way to do this writing is offered in Figure 19.

FIGURE 19

TIMES I HAVE BEEN HARMED OR
DONE HARM TO OTHERS

COLUMN 1	COLUMN 2	COLUMN 3	COLUMN 4
Situation, Cause People, Event Principals, Institution	What Happened: Specifics Why Was I: Angry? Resentful? Afraid?	What Part of Myself Was Affected? Social, Security, Sexual Instincts, Sub types	Result: My Wrongs Mistakes Faults

A sample is offered of two ways to write the information in Figure 20.

FIGURE 20

SAMPLE WRITING ON HARMS AND HURTS

TIMES I HAVE BEEN HARMED AND HURT			
Cause?	Why?	Part of Me	My Wrongs
Tim	He hit me a lot and was usually mean to me.	My body hurt. My feelings hurt. I became afraid of relationship.	I lied to myself about my feelings. I wrecked his reputation.
Tammy	I wanted to have some money and she had a lot.	My self-esteem, her property.	I stole, I lied about stealing.

There are many ways of doing this writing. Some people have written their Fourth Step inventory by going away for a weekend or two and doing it with a friend's help. Others have gone on a retreat to do this. Others have done it slowly over the space of a year, in little bits of time.

It is important to remember that even this method is only suggestive. Some people prefer a less structured approach. For this reason I include some additional methods that have also been helpful to people.

2. Be Still and Observe Yourself

In this method it is helpful to give yourself special opportunities to stroll in nature or sit in a quiet area and let yourself breathe deeply in and out. Let awareness come to you. Things will surface. As they do, write your insights about the role that anger, resentment, fears, harms, and hurts have played in your life. Remember how you responded. Write this. Insights will be gained.

3. Base Your Writing on the Enneagram.

Look at the characteristics of the Enneagram Point that seem to be most operative in your life. Look at your defect, your obsession, your sin. Look at what you pay attention to. For example, using the format of Figures 15, 17, and 19, write on conflict if you are a Nine. Write on anger, fear, depression, anything that has surfaced for you.

Let yourself look at your life and see it clearly. What has routinely drawn your attention, your focus? What has grabbed you and controlled your responses? What emotions have you experienced the most? Anger? Resentment? Fear? None? How much of a role has your Stress Point played in your life? Has it been a blessing and a resource for you? Or has your Stress Point been a place of bondage for you? Have you felt freer in your Security Point? Or, have you felt trapped by it? Write your patterns, and a new freedom will unfold for you. Look at the influence of your Wings, at their lower and higher aspects.

4. Write Down the Periods in Your Life

This strategy is helpful to be sure information is not lost in methods one, two, and three.

One way to do this writing is to decide what periods in your life are natural divisions for you.

One type of division is by the years in your life such as:

> Birth through preschool
> Elementary school
> Middle or junior high school
> High school
> College
> Jobs
> Marriages, and so forth

5. Write Down the Categories of Your Life

Another type of period division is by categories:

> Schools
> Marriages
> Jobs
> Children
> Childhood

Friends
God
Sex
Hobbies

I would like to offer a word of caution here. When you are writing your reflections, you are writing about yourself. You will be gaining invaluable insights. It is important to do this writing with a spirit of complete freedom. If you find fear creeping in about the consequences of the next Steps, go back to Steps One, Two, and Three. You are powerless. You have come to believe there is some Higher Power available to help you, even if it is only your special companion. You have made the decision to turn yourself over to the care of God as you understand this God. This includes everything you write. You are only writing right now in this Step. You are doing nothing else. No one will ever force you to do any more of these Steps. It is up to you. This is your own spiritual journey. So be at peace and keep on being open and writing. The truth will make you free.

Fourth Step Prayer

After having prepared to observe your life more specifically, and to write your inventory, you may find it helpful to begin this task with a prayer. Many people say this prayer each time they do the inventory work.

Dear _____ (However you prefer to name your Higher Power, your God), I know that I have allowed my life to be out of control in some way. I cannot undo this by myself. My mistakes are mine, and I now am beginning a searching and fearless moral inventory. I know that there are also many ways that I have done good for myself and others. I will now write my wrongs, but also the good. I pray for the courage and strength to complete this task honestly.

Having done your best to be honest and thorough in taking your Fourth Step inventory, you are now prepared to continue with Step Five.

Chapter 7

Step Five: Share Step Four With Someone

Step Five: "We admitted to God, to ourselves, and to another human being the exact nature of our wrongs."

In this Step you have already written your inventory. Now you invite another human being to be with you as you say out loud what you have learned. There are many ways to do this, but even as you talk about your life out loud, as you name your patterns, your ways of responding, you gain insights, especially if the other person has taken his or her own Step Five. To bring your awareness before God is a beautiful thing. But to bring your awareness before God and another human being, to share it, to own it in the light of life, is both beautiful and a very privileged gift. It is a special blessing to have someone love you enough to stay with you as you share this Step with him or her.

This Step helps you stop isolating. It helps you experience many profound lessons in humility. You experience a whole new sense of kinship, oneness with others and with God. This kinship opens you to a new sense of connectedness.

In this Step you share with another person what you have written. There is a saying that "you are as sick as your secrets." In this Step you let someone listen to your secrets. You have invited this person to be with you. You trust this person to be respectful without judging you. You get to experience this person listening respectfully, asking questions where necessary but staying with you to share both your strengths and weaknesses.

The person you select might be the special companion you selected earlier. It might be a spiritual director, a priest, or a minister. The important thing is that it be someone you trust to love you, to encourage you, to ask questions if something appears not to be clear, and to be discreet. What is shared is meant to be kept absolutely in confidence.

The environment is important for this sharing as well. When you feel you have done your best with Step Four, then pick an extended time for sharing it. This Step can take a very long time. It can take many hours, or even a weekend, depending on how much you have written. Be sure your companion for this understands exactly what you are asking and is able to make this special time available to you. It is very privileged time, and you deserve every minute of it.

After having shared your inventory, word by word, and each insight that might come to you, it is helpful to do some special activity to bless the occasion.

One action is to light a fire—even a small barbecue will do. Tear the papers up and let them become ashes. Let them go. Do not worry about other Steps that will come up later. Don't worry that you will forget something later on. This is a spiritual work you are doing, and your God is helping you do it!

After having prepared your inventory, you may find that it is helpful to begin Step Five with a prayer. Here is a sample prayer to use, or write your own.

Fifth Step Prayer

God, my inventory has shown me who I am. I am asking you for your help, again. I am now ready to admit my wrongs, and to share my writing with another person and with you. Please strengthen me as I take this step. With your help, I can do this, and I will do it. Amen.

Having admitted your wrongs to another person, you are now ready to begin another stage of "letting go" in Step Six.

Chapter 8

Step Six: Getting Ready to Let Go!

Step Six: "Were entirely ready to have God remove all these defects of character."

After you have shared your inventory with someone in Step Five, you have gained many insights about yourself. More action is required now. In the Twelve Steps you are always moving toward more action. You gain insights when you are on a spiritual journey. You usually feel good about this, but you have to use these insights.

You made a decision in Step Three to turn your will and your life over to the care of God as you understand this God. Now in this Step you realize that you are still a very resistant person. If you are like many others who work these Steps, you are realizing that for a long time your character defects have worked for you. Now you find yourself wondering, *"Who am I if I let go of them?"* At this stage, people have already grown a lot. They feel good. They feel wholesome, so they dig their heels in and stay at this Step.

There is a reason that this Step is separate from Step Seven. Originally, they were written as one Step, but it became clear that there was a need for a separation of Steps Six and Seven. Though little is written about it, it is perhaps the most difficult for some people.

Yes, you make a decision to turn your will and your life over to the care of God, but that numbing fear, that pervasive need to control, that avoidance of true humility, is so all pervasive! The same is true at this Step Six.

Perhaps you say, "Of course I want my character defects taken away." If this is you, then great, go for it! Pray a Sixth Step prayer with your companion and go on to Step Seven.

It is important, though, to give yourself time, if you feel in your heart that you are resistant. This is all right and normal. You never know what is behind the gate you are preparing to open on this spiritual journey, and this can be scary for you. You might feel, "If I take Step Seven and ask for my character defects to be removed, who am I going to be?"

So that you may glimpse the potential nearby and accessible to you, I include the higher or true aspects of the Enneagram Points, listed by number. These are the resources you have had available to you all along, but you did not yet have the eyes to see them. Too much damage was in the way.

You are now preparing to finish the work so that you may return (re-turn, turn again) to this better life space, your essential self. You are on a journey. What you face is a balanced life of growing much more regularly. After you surrender your "garbage," you will be able to use your gifts and skills for the good and service of others.

You will find that you will also be claiming the higher virtues and insights of your Security Point, Stress Point, and of your Wings. As you continue to grow, you will find a new freedom evolving where you will be able to call upon the gifts of each Point. You will experience a new compassion as you walk with others, as if sharing a profound communion with them.

HIGHER POINT ONE

**Perfectionist (Palmer); Reformer (Riso);
Need to Be Perfect (Rohr); Angry Virtue (Naranjo);
Inspector (Beesing, Nogosek, and O'Leary)**

Essential virtue, gift, fruit, blessing: Serenity (in the form of cheerful tranquillity)
Essential insights: Perfection (the truly good)
Description of this recovering, evolving self: Those of you in Point

One will find yourself able to put out great effort freely, being responsible, dedicated without frustration, and living with a newly found joy.

You will know the correct action to take, focusing calmly upon high standards and self-improvement, as well as assisting others to improve.

You will become more optimistic, playful, and relaxed.

You will become more comfortable with the pace of life in others and institutions, accepting life as a process with more relativity.

You will be honest and self-reliant without resentment of others. You will be critically astute, moral heroes.

HIGHER POINT TWO

Giver (Palmer); Helper (Riso)
Need to Be Needed (Rohr); Egocentric Generosity (Naranjo);
Assistant (Beesing, Nogosek, and O'Leary

Essential virtue, gift, fruit, blessing: Humility
Essential insights: Freedom of your will
Description of this recovering, evolving self: Those of you in Point Two will be able to convey a willingness to give help if it is needed, with no expectation of return.

You will be able to recognize your own needs humbly without exaggerating or minimizing them.

You will be able to feel your own feelings, accepting the anxiety of this, affirming yourself as good.

You will be able help people to feel good about themselves, drawing out the best in others.

You will be able to remain in relationships, keeping them alive and meaningful, and you will be happy to honor celebrations important to the life of others.

You will become free to feel your anger and to communicate it effectively to others, letting go of it and living with peace.

You will become less dependent, able to rely upon your own strengths.

HIGHER POINT THREE

Performer, Do-er (Palmer); Status Seeker (Riso);
Need to Succeed (Rohr);
Success through Appearances (Naranjo);
Administrator (Beesing, Nogosek, and O'Leary)

Essential virtue, gift, fruit, blessing: Honesty
Essential insights: Confidence and hope
Description of this recovering, evolving self: Those of you in Point Three will find that you are able to remain loyal to your best self and to your friends.

You will be able to live with healthy doubt and personal humility, rather than activity.

You will be able to view yourself as other than your role.

You will be able to be comfortable with the poor, the needy, the commonness in others, in work, and in yourself.

Your infectious enthusiasm will be clearly focused for projects and goals, yet you will have a profoundly grounded knowledge that you are separate from the project.

You will find an ease in encouraging personal growth and excellence in others.

You will relish your own lifelong learning and take a renewed interest in life.

HIGHER POINT FOUR

Tragic-Romantic (Palmer); Artist (Riso);
Need to Be Special (Rohr);
Seeking Happiness Through Pain (Naranjo);
Author (Beesing, Nogosek, and O'Leary)

Essential virtue, gift, fruit, blessing: Connection to one's original
source
Essential insights: Sense of harmony, balance in life
Description of this recovering, evolving self: Those of you in Point Four will find yourself embracing a sense of connectedness and peace

within yourself. This will come and go, but it will be experienced more and more regularly. You will sense a connectedness to something that is not there but is bigger than yourself, possibly even your original source, your deeper Higher Power.

You will continue to know the sense of being pulled within but will come to know a sense of balance with the outer life as well. You will come to know that what you have is what you really need. You will come to be able to accept the present and focus with peace on life as it is, "right here, right now."

You will deepen in your capacity to be sensitive to your own feelings and to the feelings of others.

You will be able to be empathetic with others because of your own suffering. You will want to help others because of your own journey.

Life will become for you an experience of rich meaning and pure quality.

You will deepen in your qualities of being passionate, idealistic, and creative.

You will be able to be comfortably assertive, content to work to change situations for the better.

You will lose your feelings of inferiority and of clinging to others for happiness. Instead, you will grow to become comfortable in your ability to say no to helping, if you feel the need to do so.

HIGHER POINT FIVE

Observer (Palmer); Thinker (Riso);
Need to Perceive (Rohr);
Seeking Wholeness Through Isolation (Naranjo)
Sage (Beesing, Nogosek, and O'Leary)

Essential virtue, gift, fruit, blessing: Detachment
Essential insights: Wisdom (knowing deeply, clearly)
Description of this recovering, evolving self: Those of you who are in Point Five will be able to transform your previously false sense of detachment by which you lived.

You will become open to feelings, desires, and the sense of not having enough. You will be open to accepting a full range of feelings.

You will accept impressions, remaining able to let them go freely.

Instead of holding on to that which you know in a self-protective way, you will begin to share what you know. You will be able to merge what you know with other bodies of knowledge. You will become able to integrate knowledge and experiences in the past and the present for a balanced, integrated present and future.

You will be able to focus on difficult decisions, detaching them from your own fears and desires.

You will then be able to concentrate on theoretical, behind-the-scenes work, to study with peace and skill. This will be scholarly and thoughtfully done.

You will become integrated within yourself, your mind, emotions, sexuality, and your body, experiencing new health, wholeness, and energy.

HIGHER POINT SIX

Devil's Advocate (Palmer); Loyalist (Riso);
Need for Security/ Certainty (Rohr);
Persecuted Persecutor (Naranjo);
Facilitator (Beesing, Nogosek, and O'Leary)

Essential virtue, gift, fruits, blessing: Courage
Essential insights: Faith and trust
Description of this recovering, evolving self: Those of you who are in Point Six will trust your instincts, becoming more capable of trusting others.

You will become able to live as integrated people, reducing the use of the mind as only a negative filter.

You will become free to act, with your body and heart becoming strong partners with your strongly capable mind.

You will become able to focus your attention on "the good" in life, the truthful, your own and others' positive experiences. You will focus less on questioning, fears, and doubts.

You will also become thoughtful, warm, protective, and devoted to others.

You will trust yourself and this new instinct as your faith deepens. You will allow for your intuition to develop, becoming more capable of accepting good ideas from your own experiences as well as from others.

You will be able to serve others in the name of duty with confidence and abiding loyalty.

You will become able to experience your own hurts, suffering, and sacrifice with honesty, but to serve again with peace and confidence without cynicism or fear.

HIGHER POINT SEVEN

Epicure or Planner (Palmer); Generalist (Riso);
Need to Avoid Pain (Rohr); Opportunistic Idealism (Naranjo);
Optimist (Beesing, Nogosek, and O'Leary)

Essential virtue, gift, fruit, blessing: Sobriety (sober joy)
Essential insights: Work, cooperation with God
Description of this recovering, evolving self: When those of you in Point Seven develop this new level of awareness in your life, you find that you accept each moment for whatever it is offering, whether this is joyful or sad, boring or stimulating.

You become able to remain in jobs, in situations, and in relationships. You do not have to leave them, to have diversions or stimulating secondary plans, in order to avoid boredom.

You become able to remain committed to a course of action without being afraid to slow down. You can live with boredom and pain without fear.

You will be happy, joyful, playful, enjoying life and becoming enjoyable to be around.

You will then find a renewed capacity to be inventive, imaginative, and even more energetic.

You will find a powerfully new deeper optimism toward others and toward life in general.

HIGHER POINT EIGHT

Boss (Palmer); Leader (Riso);
Need to Be Against (Rohr); Coming on Strong (Naranjo);
Champion (Beesing, Nogosek, and O'Leary)

Essential virtue, gift, fruit, blessing: Innocence
Essential insights: Truth, compassion (mercy)
Description of this recovering, evolving self: Those of you in Point Eight will be able to recognize truth in the actions of others and in situations. You will become secure enough to be able to interact, dropping your defenses on a regular and comfortable basis.

You will find that fear is less familiar to you.

You will also find that compromise becomes easier.

You will be comfortable in situations without any advance ideas or expectations of what will be expected of you. You will also get to experience a comfortable sense of personal confidence.

You become aware of the energy you project and will know intuitively how to modify it as needed in a variety of situations.

You will see yourself receiving the life perceptions and experiences of others with openness and compassion, rather than with arrogance, confusion, and judgment.

You will then find yourself responding consistently to continuous pressure with focus, attention, and gentleness.

You will be comfortable remaining committed to projects and will be content to serve in positions requiring you to protect those in need of your care and support.

As this develops, you will become surprised at your newly found capacity to be simultaneously just, friendly, truthful, straightforward, and clear.

You will relate helpfully to others, presenting yourself simply and generously.

You will become comfortable with acknowledging the needs and sensitivities within yourself.

HIGHER POINT NINE

Mediator (Palmer); Peacemaker (Riso);
Need to Avoid (Rohr); Going With the Stream (Naranjo);
Negotiator (Beesing, Nogosek, and O'Leary)

Essential virtue, gift, fruit, blessing: Right action
Essential insights: Unconditional love
Description of this recovering, evolving self: Those of you who identify with Point Nine will find yourself accepting yourself as good.

You will become able to stand inside your own skin and reach out
to others with genuine love and affection.

You will become able to perceive what is the correct thing to do,
the "right action" to take, the project to focus upon.

You will become able to focus, not to become distracted by the
inessential, and be able to stay committed to work on the task you
have selected until it is completed.

You will observe yourself listening to others with respect, without
judging the positions of others or feeling the need to alter your own
stance.

You will become free to be caring and attentive to others, giving
generously without compromising yourself, your positions, your own
goals.

You will experience a new comfort at being accountable to others
and able to participate in activities with them.

You will find your ability to sense the essential in others' lives greatly
enhanced. This will enable you to identify with what is crucial for them
in a supportive way, without sacrificing your own essence.

You will come to experience yourself as alive, self-competent, able
to turn conflicts into constructive opportunities for growth and development for yourself and others.

Figure 21 presents a summary of these essential higher aspects, fruits,
gifts, blessings, and insights of the nine Points.

FIGURE 21

ENNEAGRAM POINTS: HIGHER
TRAITS, VIRTUES, FRUITS,
GIFTS, BLESSINGS

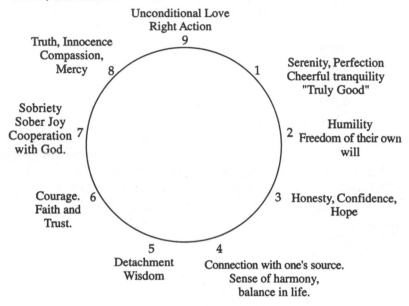

Unconditional Love
Right Action
9

Truth, Innocence
Compassion,
Mercy 8

Serenity, Perfection
Cheerful tranquility
"Truly Good"
1

Sobriety
Sober Joy
Cooperation 7
with God.

Humility
Freedom of their own
will
2

Courage. 6
Faith and
Trust.

Honesty, Confidence,
Hope
3

5
Detachment
Wisdom

4
Connection with one's source.
Sense of harmony,
balance in life.

Helps to Take Step Six

There are strategies you can use to help yourself through this Step.
I will present some of these as possibilities, if you should find a need for
them within yourself.

1. List Your Feelings and Thoughts

Make a list of your present feelings and thoughts. What is going on
for you specifically? What is holding you back from being ready to let
go of your character defects, your traits, obsession, sin?

2. Write a Letter

Write a letter to yourself or to God or to a friend. Let the pen or
pencil just move along the paper.

Include what you think you would have to let go of if you take Steps Six and Seven. Write down how you feel about this. Include those character aspects you would like to keep as resources within you. How do you feel about this? Write your feelings.

Write a letter to your emotions. Write down how you have treated yourself in your life. Write down how you have let others treat you.

Write down how you have engaged in play in your life. Do the same for your work.

Write down how you have engaged in a relationship with your God. How have you prayed, depended upon God?

Write down what is holding you back from being willing to let go of your character defects. What is going on that is holding you back from being open to take on the new higher aspects of your new essential self?

3. Share Your Writing With Someone

Having done the previous steps, now share this writing with someone, maybe your special companion. Read it out loud. Let yourself be, embracing how you are now. Do not judge yourself. You will become ready in time.

4. Ask for God's Help

Write a prayer or make one up spontaneously. Ask to let go of any resistance you may feel within you. A sample prayer is offered below, if it is helpful for you. Pray it with your special companion, a friend, your priest or your minister.

Sixth Step Prayer

Dear _____ (However you call your God or Higher Power), I do not want to hang on to my personality fixations and patterns that do not serve you or others. I now see myself more honestly than I did before. I want to let go and open up to the higher, better ways that you are offering to me. I now feel ready to surrender myself to you and your role in my life. Amen.

Congratulations, you are now ready to move on and to take Step Seven.

Chapter 9

Step Seven: Let Go!

Step Seven: "Humbly asked Him to remove our short-comings."

Sometimes people will feel a fervor and readiness after Step Six. But they slip back and forget to take Step Seven. They skip on to Eight through Twelve. Each of us fights humility! It is the hardest part of the spiritual journey—to continue to "let God be God." You can do this Step quickly, right away, after taking Step Six. You can pray the Seventh Step prayer of your choice, or the one offered in this section. Or you can realize that you are still at Step Six and not yet ready for Step Seven.

I know of others who have tried to use will power, or "positive imaging," instead of taking this Step. You make mental images of the new behaviors you want to have, as if you are still "in charge." Positive imaging and affirmation are good strategies, but they are not appropriate for the purposes of Step Seven.

You will have plenty of time for strategies to help yourself affirm and practice new behaviors for the rest of your life, but for now it is time to admit your powerlessness again and to ask God to remove your shortcomings. You don't need to say which shortcomings, just let God take over. God knows far more than you do. (Of course, you are free to ask for specific characteristics to be taken away, if you want to do so.)

Do not be fooled by the fact that the commentary in this section on Step Seven is so brief. This is a hard step too! This Step is a blow to the ego because you must admit again in a deeper way that you need to change. You admit you can't do this by yourself. You admit you need God to break the chains that bind you. As you will experience, this Step will free you from the trap of pride and fear.

Little by little, after you take this Step, you will find yourself thinking differently, feeling differently, and responding differently. People and the situations around you will seem to change, and so will your responses to them.

When you feel you are ready, begin to take Step Seven by expressing a prayer of your choice, or the one suggested below from the book of *Alcoholics Anonymous*.

Seventh Step Prayer

My Creator, I am now willing that you should have all of me, good and bad. I pray that you now remove from me every single defect of character which stands in the way of my usefulness to you and my fellows. Grant me strength, as I go out from here, to do your bidding. Amen.[4]

Chapter 10

Step Eight: Look Again at Your Behavior

Step Eight: "Made a list of all persons we had harmed, and became willing to make amends to them all."

This Step is unique. You might expect that you would make a list of all those who had harmed you and then go to beat them up, or focus on trying to forgive them. This is not the direction that you take in the Twelve Steps or in the Enneagram. Your task is to observe yourself and "your side of the tennis court," so to speak. Somehow, the miracle that evolves is that when you clean up your messes, you find yourself forgiving the injustices, the harms done to you, much more easily.

The essential point of Step Eight is that you focus on the resentments, fears, harms, and hurts of your life by paying attention to *your* responses. You will be able to remember what you need to remember. You will focus on the material of column 4 of the Fourth Step inventory. What were your responses to the situations, events, and people you described?

As you shared your Fifth Step, you became aware of ways in which your responses might have "needed improvement," or perhaps you were outright vindictive! What you do now is to write down those to whom *you* owe amends.

This Step is best taken with another person to help you to be thorough, to help you not to hide yourself, not to isolate, and not to be too hard on yourself. Again, if this becomes scary for you, perhaps there is a need to look again at how badly you want this growth. Ask yourself again if you have really taken the Steps leading up to this one. Look at the quality of your surrender and trust, and the reality of your Seventh Step.

This Eighth Step can be really scary. Sometimes you say, "Oh no, no way!" "I'll never make an amends to that S.O.B.!" Well, fine! No one says you have to do so, not now, and not later. Your Higher Power will lead you on a journey for a long time to come. Just stay open. If you don't want to write someone's name down, then don't do it. It is your journey, not mine, and nobody else's. If your special companion suggests something, this is still for you to decide, though it might be good to try to be open to this person's input. If others tell you to write something, they might be meeting their own needs which are not in your best interests. Just continue to ask your God to touch your heart, and this will be done.

It is important to remember that you are only making a list at this time. No other action is being taken at this Step. Right now you are continuing to work on clearing away the wreckage of your past. You are preparing to restore a healthy state, a balance for yourself, but also for others. In this Step you are not actually making any amends (restitution) to anyone, but you are preparing to do so.

It is important not to do all of the Step alone. Sometimes you have an eagerness when you experience the new life found through Steps One through Seven. You have the enthusiasm called "first fervor," and you might just rush in to Step Nine, to confess, to say you are sorry. You could possibly injure yourself or others in your zeal, even though your heart is in the right place. Your intentions may be good, but it is very important to share your amends list with a trusted friend or your special companion and talk about the best ways to proceed.

Strategies for Doing Step Eight

1. Ask for Guidance First

It can be very threatening to even think about making amends to others. In order to be as strong as possible in doing this, it helps to ask God to come into your heart and mind to help you.

To do this, say a prayer or write one. If it is helpful for you, use the sample prayer at the end of this chapter.

2. Make an Amends List

A suggested way to prepare your list is shown in Figure 22. You could use a form such as in Figure 22, or just take a piece of paper. Fold it in half lengthwise, and put the person, institution, or group name on the left and the reason on the right. Use as much paper as you need. No need to skimp here.

FIGURE 22

SAMPLE AMENDS LIST

NAME OF PERSON INSTITUTION, GROUP	REASON FOR AMENDS
Susan	I stole $500 from her
Myself	I blamed myself often when I did not deserve this.

To use this method, take a piece of paper, 8 1/2 x 11 inches. Draw two columns. In column 1 list the name of the person or institution you may have harmed or hurt. In column 2 write the reason that an amends is necessary. Write down what you did that you believe was selfish, dishonest, self-seeking, a result of fear, or inconsiderate. These can be words or actions that you did, but not feelings or thoughts you may have had. Feelings are only feelings, and thoughts are only thoughts. How you act upon them is what you are responsible for.

3. Revised Amends List

A suggested way to prepare your revised amends list is shown in Figure 23.

FIGURE 23

REVISED AMENDS LIST

NAME	A			B	C
Person, Institution, or Group	Type of Phone	Possible Visit	Contact Letter	Can't Do	Won't

A: Those to whom you will make amends by phone, letter, in person.
B: Those you cannot find.
C: Those who are dead, or you chose not to make direct amends to them.

Look at your first "Amends List" with your special companion. Look at it carefully. Now take another piece of paper, possibly 8 1/2 x 11 inches. Divide it into three columns as shown in Figure 23. The first column is for the name of the person or institution deserving amends.

Column A will be for those you will decide to make amends to. You decide the best way to try to make your amends. This would be by phone, visit, letter (written correspondence).

Column B will be for those you cannot find. You discuss some other action you might take to make up for your wrongs, if this might be possible to do.

Column C will be for those to whom you cannot make amends either because they are dead or because you decide this would injure them or another or yourself.

As you work on this "Revised Amends List," other names might come to mind. Continue to add them to your list.

Basically, this is all there is to taking Step Eight. No direct amends is necessary. This is for Step Nine.

Eighth Step Prayer

Dear _____(God, or whoever you call your Higher Power), I ask your help as I make my list of those whom I have harmed. Help me to be rigorously honest and willing, as I prepare to make restitution for what I have done and for that which I have failed to do. Amen

Having made your list to the best of your ability, you are now ready to do the action of Step Nine.

Chapter 11

Step Nine: Find Ways to Make Amends

Step Nine: "Made direct amends to such people wherever possible, except when to do so would injure them or others."

After making your list in Step Eight, you now move into the action stage of making your amends. When you actually do the work of Step Nine, you will be surprised at the responses of those whom you approach to make amends. On the whole you will find that people, businesses, and institutions are very accepting. However, a word of caution. You are not making your amends so that people will pat you on the back. Some people may not be gracious and kind. This can make you angry, but it is your responsibility to do your amends from your inventory. It is not your task to take others' inventory or to judge them and what amends they need to be making to you. Your task here is to focus only upon the areas you can do something about: yourself and your actions.

You do not want to act in such a way that you will later see a need to add this person's name again, because you acted defensively, rudely, or in an attacking way. Your responsibility is to speak simply and address your error and the part you played in the harm that's been done. If the person does not give you the opportunity to do this, then so be it. You have at least tried! This is enough. You do not need to force your amends upon others.

It may trouble you that you have not been able to make necessary restitution. Most people are able to figure out some alternative action to take by praying on this. Discuss the matter with your special companion. Do what you can and then let go of the matter. An analogy might help you understand what is happening here.

Picture yourself playing ping-pong or tennis. If you really practice this game, you can control the way the ball goes over the net. You can control the speed and the position it goes to. You can influence your opponent's game by your posture, your attitude, and your gestures. You cannot control exactly how your opponent hits the ball, exactly where it goes, or his attitude or gestures.

The same principle holds for your Twelve Step journey and your amends. You do your best. You lob the ball over and pray you will receive the ball that is lobbed back to you.

I would like to offer a few words of encouragement at this point. You will probably find someone near the top of your amends list who is going to be someone very close to you. You need to be really open to making all of your amends. It will take time to find the right, best way to do this, but share with your special companion and stay open to learning how to proceed.

The person whom you have harmed the most is *yourself*! Be kind to yourself. You deserve it. One approach to do this is offered as a suggestion in the discussion of Step Nine.

Strategies for Doing Step Nine

1. Ask for Guidance and Strength

Before beginning the action of making the amends, it is very helpful to bring your God into the process. Ask for help simply. If you feel more comfortable preparing a prayer, do so. A sample Ninth Step prayer is offered at the end of this chapter.

2. Write Yourself Some Amends Letters

As a strategy to make amends to yourself, write yourself some letters. You will possibly feel strange doing this, but let yourself feel! You have probably put it off long enough. By putting the pen to the paper, or the fingers to the keyboard, you unlock a door that leads to many new understandings, insights, and healing.

Write a letter to your body. Even if it feels foolish, you are the one writing it and reading it. The person you might share it with will be kind and understanding, or maybe you'll just share it with yourself. It's up to you.

List what you've done to hurt yourself, your body. Write down the reason. Perhaps you abused it sexually or allowed this to be done to it. Perhaps you abused it by imbalances and sickness you've allowed to develop as consequences of your behavior. Perhaps you overate or underate. Perhaps you overworked or underworked and didn't get the rest or exercise you needed. Praise what is good and resilient about your body. Thank it and apologize. Offer a reward to your body by way of restitution. Give it some massages, a membership in a weight program, a spa to help rebuild that which you helped to tear down.

Write a letter to your mind. Include the times you just "shut down" on thinking. Include when you used your mind to avoid fear, anger, and anxiety. List the ways you imprisoned your mind through your choice of reading, of friends. List the people to whom you gave authority to do your thinking for you. Write down if you lied to yourself or others, denying or inflating your talents. Write down if you imprisoned your mind by narcotizing (overdosing) through your use of television, food, alcohol, and drugs. Praise what is good and resilient about your mind. Thank it and apologize.

Write a letter to your feelings. Admit honestly the times you have denied them, belittled them, ignored them. Write down how you have let others belittle them. Write down how you have shoved them down (imprisoned them), by overeating or undereating, by the use of alcohol, drugs, television, or other distractions. Write down if you have restricted them to the world of your mind or fantasy instead of nurturing them through the work of real relationships. Praise what is good and resilient about your feelings. Thank them and apologize.

In each letter perhaps you could also write what you would like to do differently. Go back to Step Six on this, and then take Step Seven if necessary.

3. Make the Amends from Your Revised Amends List

Go back to your Revised Amends List from Step Eight. You have agreed to take specific action with your special companion. All that remains is to do it. May your journey be blessed.

Ninth Step Prayer

Dear _____ (However you call your Higher Power, your idea of God), I pray for the right attitude to make my amends well. I pray to make these amends in a way that will not harm others. Please help me in those areas where I need to make indirect amends by helping others and growing in spiritual progress.

You do not need to be finished with Step Nine to begin to take Step Ten. Your Step Nine amends can take a long time, but if you are working on them, you are ready to continue to Step Ten.

Chapter 12

Step Ten: Ongoing Maintenance Is a Must

Step Ten: "Continued to take personal inventory and when we were wrong promptly admitted it."

For your spiritual revolution to continue, you need to remain ready to work at it. Step Ten is really a daily, weekly, monthly, and annual review of Steps Two through Nine. It has been said that Step Ten consists of Step One through Step Nine because we must always remember our powerlessness lest we forget the place of God in our lives. Some say that for them this Step consists of Steps Two through Nine. Regardless of the view, what you do is walk each Step briefly on a daily basis.

There are many ways and resources available for you to use in this Step. One is to allow your dreams to happen, to write them down, to "mull over" your meaning with your special companion. Another is to be faithful to writing in a notebook of some sort, a "Mini-Fourth Step," a summary of the good and the not-so-good of the day, to share it, then to do Steps Six, Seven, Eight, and Nine with what you learn. The more you do this, the easier and more comfortable it becomes.

By now you have become aware of the characteristics of your personality. You have observed yourself, your Enneagram Point, and the subtleties of how you have lived.

In Step Ten, you take a "mini-review" of the day. You take a look at the character gifts you have shared with yourself and with others today. Take a look at what caused you stress and how you responded. You get to look at the good and the not-so-good. You write it down.

Some people call this *journaling*. Others prefer just to call it taking Step Ten. It does make a big difference, though, to pick up the pen and write. This really does free the mind and the heart.

It is almost as if you are on a journey, so you write in your diary about the trip. Where amends need to be made, you say "oops," and you do what you have to do to get "back on track." If you have really had a horrible day and felt you "blew it" or "lost your cool" or withdrew when you should have "held your place," you need to be patient with yourself. On this journey it is very important to remain in constant contact with your special companion.

When things are tough for you, this does not mean you have failed. It means you have another growth opportunity. In the Twelve Step literature it is regularly encouraged that you keep an ongoing communication open with your special companion. When the going gets tough, it is all the more important to dig in, to focus, and to "get going." There is a saying, "When the going gets tough, the tough get going."

In Step Ten you talk about what is going on in your life. If there is a need to do so, you make your amends quickly. There are repeated encouraging statements in the literature to remind you that you don't have to walk this journey perfectly. Your feet twist and the path has unexpected turns, so you go near the edge. The goal is "Spiritual Progress, not Spiritual Perfection."[5]

Practices to Help You With Step Ten

1. Mini-inventory List

In this method take paper. It can be in your diary notebook or small scratch pad or regular typewriter size. Do what feels comfortable.

Make two columns as seen in Figure 24.

In column 1 write what comes to mind when you think of the character assets, gifts, virtues, and blessings you practiced during the day.

In column 2 write the character defects that surfaced during the day but that you feel have outlived their usefulness.

FIGURE 24

MINI-INVENTORY LIST

TODAY I PRACTICED	
These Character Gifts, Virtues, Blessings	These Character Defects, Obsessions, Wrongs

After making your list, thank God for the good, and take Steps One through Nine on the rest. I will give an example of how you could do this.

Step One: Yes, the defect surfaced, and I admit that I was powerless over it.

Step Two: I let myself reflect upon the fact that, yes, I slipped. I stumbled, but a power greater than myself could restore me to the balance that was happening.

Step Three: I make a decision to try again, to let go and to let God be God for me in my life. I am ready to accept the help I need that is being extended to me.

Step Four: Next, I jot down a mini-reflection on what happened. Where was I? Who was involved? What happened? What feelings were occurring? What Enneagram traits were occurring? What was my response to this? How did I do?

Step Five: In a call or a visit with my special companion, I share what I have written or the insights I have gained.

Step Six: I pray to be ready to let go of whatever has surfaced.

Step Seven: I ask God to remove this trait at a deeper level and to use you for the service of others as they need.

Step Eight: I write down the name of the person or group or institution to whom I might be owing amends. I include the reason and how I might go about this. I share this with my special companion.

Step Nine: I make the amends that I have agreed are appropriate and necessary.

Step Ten: I continue to take a personal inventory, and when I have wronged others, I admit this promptly.

2. A Quicker Mini-inventory

As you practice these Steps as principles to live by on a daily basis, you will find that your awareness and self-observation skills will become much more effective and much quicker. The task is to take this Step! The method doesn't matter. Some people take a "Mini-Tenth Step" several times a day. Others make amends as soon as they see that they have erred. It is good, though, to keep in contact with your special companion and to keep the habit of making notes on paper. (Some people report that they don't use pen or paper but the computer for journaling. This is fine, too, if it is helpful for you. Just stay open and honest.

3. Characteristics Lists

Another strategy that is helpful is to make your own list of those personality characteristics that you no longer practice. You have asked that they be removed from you. What remains is allowing for the awareness of the practice of your new habits and thoughts. A sample way to do this was offered in Figure 24. Develop your own list. The list for each Enneagram Point will be different.

The list made by each person within the same Point will be unique because an individual is always changing. This is because each one of you is working on unique traits with more focus than others at any given time. Character traits and patterns that you worked on at one time in your program might not need the same attention at another time. More is revealed to you as you continue to walk this journey. As with any trip that you take, the vistas change. It is also helpful to look at your list and evaluate what could be added or dropped.

For example, as you become less self-centered, you will find that you become more sensitive to the needs of others. You are then able to listen to your feelings lovingly, with gentle compassion and without many arrogant, self-righteous judgments. You're getting better. You notice that what you need to concentrate on now is not so much control of a specific person or control in conversations. You are growing in becoming more compassionate and sensitive to others. What you need to concentrate on right now is your part in helping with the development of the quality of life of others. Right now you need to look at how you use your society's resources in ways that hurt other people. You need to look at the amount of beef you think you are entitled to. You know now that this habit of consumption is affecting the air you breathe, the land, the crop supply for many others. Perhaps you can use less fuel by making fewer trips or organizing a car pool. You might not need to use the amount of electricity and gas that you use.

You might never put these reflections on your list, but someone else might need to do this. The point is to stay open and listen to your God in your heart.

To make your list, look at the Enneagram Points. Write down those habits of attention and passions, the character traits that are of concern for you. Write the emotions that dominate you. On the right side of the paper write the virtues and higher aspects of the mind that you feel you want to begin to live or to deepen in. It is the rhythm of your own heart that must be heeded. Share this list as you prepare it with your special friend. You might want to add something or you might agree that for now, it is better to leave it off the list.

Every day, or at least periodically, look at your list to see how you are doing. Write about it. Share this. Take the action where necessary to right any wrong you may have done. Thank God for the good you have been doing. Thank God for the good you have become.

Figure 25 summarizes the lower traits, defects, obsessions, of the Enneagram Points for your use as a possible reference.

FIGURE 25

THE ENNEAGRAM LOWER
TRAITS, DEFECTS, OBSESSIONS,
"SIN"

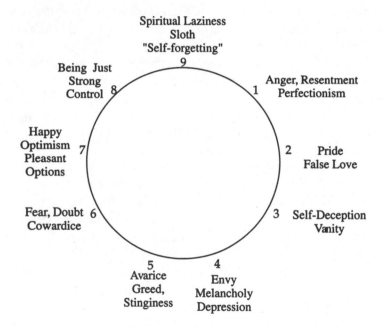

Figure 26 summarizes the Enneagram subtypes. This is offered as a resource to assist you in observing what is happening. It can be very helpful to self-observe to see what basic instincts and subtypes you are relying upon.

FIGURE 26

THE ENNEAGRAM
INSTINCTS/SUBTYPES

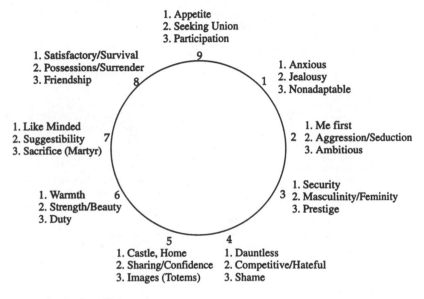

1. Appetite
2. Seeking Union
3. Participation

1. Satisfactory/Survival
2. Possessions/Surrender
3. Friendship

1. Anxious
2. Jealousy
3. Nonadaptable

1. Like Minded
2. Suggestibility
3. Sacrifice (Martyr)

1. Me first
2. Aggression/Seduction
3. Ambitious

1. Warmth
2. Strength/Beauty
3. Duty

1. Security
2. Masculinity/Feminity
3. Prestige

1. Castle, Home
2. Sharing/Confidence
3. Images (Totems)

1. Dauntless
2. Competitive/Hateful
3. Shame

Instinctions (Subtypes)

1. Self-preservation survival
2. One-one, sexual
3. Social, group

To use the Enneagram as a mirror, look at how you are operating when you are experiencing stress. Are you operating out of the lower aspects of your Stress Point or the Security Point?

When you are feeling wholesome and strong, perhaps you are operating out of higher aspects of your own Point or of the Security Point or even the Stress Point. It is helpful to stop and look. This is the invitation of Step Ten. Figures 27 and 28 present summaries of the "inclination to act" when we are experiencing what we perceive as stress or security.

FIGURE 27

THE ENNEAGRAM AND THE STRESS POINTS

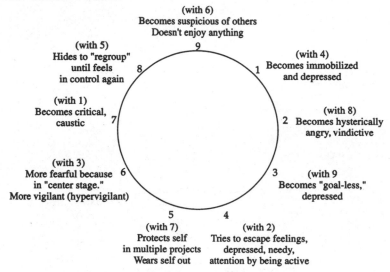

FIGURE 28

THE ENNEAGRAM AND THE SECURITY POINTS

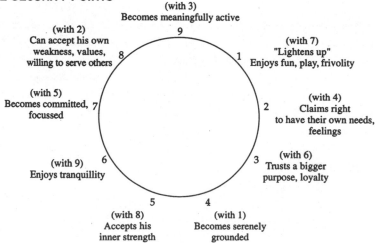

4. The H.A.L.T. Reminder

A very easy way to know if you are bordering on "slipping" back into your earlier patterns, your "trap," is to check yourself out with four simple words. Your first letters spell the word *halt*. The key words are *hungry, angry, lonely, and tired*. If you are letting yourself become too hungry, too angry, too lonely, or too tired, you might be moving into the slippery area that makes for regression. You might find yourself slipping into past patterns, past defects, unless you shift gears. It is very important to take care of yourself first and the rest will fall into place.

5. Use the Skills of Professionals

The Twelve Step literature is very specific that more will be revealed to you little by little.[6] Some people find that as part of Tenth Step growth they have a need to use other resources, too. This is good and is to be encouraged. Sometimes people say, "What's wrong with my program? Maybe I'm not working the Steps right. Maybe I'm not being open in how I observe myself."

It is very possible that nothing is wrong with your "program." It may very well be that you are working your program very well. It can simply be that you are listening to what is going on. Pain is happening in your life. You need more help and support at this time, that's all. You are very much alive! Congratulations!

The Twelve Step literature encourages you to avail yourself of professionals and other resources if these are helpful for you.[7] They are there for you. You have the right to listen to your needs. As this occurs, be honest with your special companion, then go ahead and work with these resource people until you do not need to do so. You might need more assistance to change your habits of caring for your body. You might need some massage, some weight-reduction (or weight-gaining) assistance, some training in a martial art so as to come into partnership with your body. You might need help letting yourself stay with your feelings and learning from them no matter how difficult this can become.

Psychological assistance might be needed to do this. You might need formally structured opportunities such as courses to retrain the mind or to free the artistic gifts within.

In her book *The Enneagram*,[8] Palmer describes the help that persons in various Points have found to be helpful. There are also many workshops and courses available to help you learn what each Point has experienced as helpful. Additional resources are included in the Resources section (Appendix One) of this book.

6. Inner Symptoms Checklist

Bernie Siegel offers a checklist to use as a type of temperature taking. He lists symptoms of inner peace. If many of these are occurring in your life, then you are doing well. Siegel would caution, however, "If you have all or even most of these symptoms, please be advised that your Condition of Peace may be so far advanced as to not be treatable."[9]

- Tendency to think and act spontaneously rather than from fears based on past experiences.
- An unmistakable ability to enjoy each moment.
- Loss of interest in judging self.
- Loss of interest in judging other people.
- Loss of interest in conflict.
- Loss of interest in interpreting the actions of others.
- Loss of the ability to worry.
- Frequent, overwhelming episodes of appreciation.
- Contented feelings of connectedness with others and nature.
- Frequent attacks of smiling through the eyes of the heart.
- Increasing susceptibility to love extended by others as well as the uncontrollable urge to extend it.
- Increasing tendency to let things happen rather than to make them happen.

Tenth Step Prayer

As with each of the Twelve Steps, it is helpful to remain connected with your Higher Power, your God, asking for help to take each Step carefully and honestly. Below is a suggested prayer, though the form of your expression may just as well be a gesture, a word, or other words.

Dear _____ (the name you choose to call your Higher Power), I pray for your help that I may continue to take the daily inventory of my life. Help me to correct my mistakes when I make them. Help me to take responsibility for my actions, to continue to be open to see my self-defeating traps and behaviors.

Help me to remember that I need your help to keep love and tolerance of others as my code.

In closing, remember that remaining faithful to this Step leads you very naturally into the next step, Step Eleven.

Chapter 13

Step Eleven: Keeping Contact With Your Source

Step Eleven: "Sought through prayer and meditation to improve our conscious contact with God as we understood Him, praying only for knowledge of His will for us and the power to carry that out."

As you took the earlier Steps, and as you work Step Eleven, you find that everything else in your life seems to be just "falling into place." You work this Step as a humble, empty vessel who knows your need for God.

In this Step an awakening happens that leads you to hunger after holiness (wholeness) in all areas of your life. Your emotions become balanced. Your body seeks proper rhythms of rest, work, and play, and the right food and drink. You hunger for a sharing of peace and reconciliation in your relationships and in the world.

You find yourself led deeply to the roots of your spiritual life. You recognize that you are craving a personally meaningful contact with your God. Eventually, you find yourself with a hunger to share religious expression with others. You find that you want to search out your religious life in a new, adult way.

In Step Eleven you do background preparation. You take the time to be still, to listen to your God in your life, and to receive insights for your life. There are many resources available for you to use in this Step. I offer some of these in the hope that they may be of help.

Some Practices for Step Eleven

1. Meditation as Following the Breath

When we first discussed the Enneagram in the Introduction, you saw that there are three centers out of which you operate: the gut, the head, and the heart. Your predominant passions, sin, and habits of paying attention come from there, as do your recovery and growth.

In the practice of meditation you prepare first by selecting a special space to use and set aside for prayer. It is good to decide how long you want to stay at this. If you are beginning to meditate, or returning to it after a time away, try this for only five minutes at a time. After a while you will want to move to ten or twenty minutes.

Let yourself sit comfortably on the floor or on a chair. Sit so that the spine is comfortable yet straight. Close your eyes. Slowly breathe in through the nose. Slowly breathe out through the nose or mouth. Do whichever is most comfortable for you.

Pay attention. Follow the breath. With your mind watch it come in, turn down the spine into the gut, then up into the chest and head. As you watch the breath, watch it healing, giving life, bringing in a new spirit. Imagine that you are breathing in security and breathing out calm. If thoughts come, let them come and go fondly. Don't fight or push them away. Just follow the breath and trust that you will be renewed. It will happen. You will receive insights.

Some people report that they even set a timer for their five or ten minutes so that they don't have to watch their watches. This is fine. The only thing that is important is to let yourself focus as you begin, and do some gesture or breathing as your last step in this process.

2. Meditation as Centering Prayer

Find a special place. Select a comfortable position. Sit on the floor or on a chair. Lie flat on your back. Some people even walk very slowly, concentrating on each step.

Some prefer no sounds or scents. Others find relaxation or meditative music or chants as background for their meditation. Some prefer incense. Some prefer to say a sentence, a phrase, or word over and over. Some read a poem or a Scripture text before beginning their meditation.

Try a variety of ways to do this. You will be led to find what is most helpful for you.

Breathe in, and let the breath go to your center: the heart, the head (actually, imagine the breath going to the back of the forehead as if to a third eye), or to the gut (just below the belly button). Stay with this breathing. Breathe slowly, focusing on the breath in and out. Breathe slowly, quietly, with your mind and heart repeating a selected word, a phrase, or a sentence.

Set a timer if you wish, but allow for gradual closing of the practice. Meditation is a very simple thing to do, but it is very profound. You can jar yourself if you stop too abruptly.

3. Meditation as Reflective Reading

Select a special place and time. This can be in your home, church, car, but try to be consistent. Relax. Be comfortable. Now pick up the text you have chosen. Many people select from a variety of books, inspirational reading, and Scripture.

Read slowly, then be still. Be ready to receive whatever insights might come. If you feel a need to work with some of the feelings that surfaced, write them down and let yourself comment on what you think is going on. It is also helpful to share this with your special companion.

4. Meditation as Contemplation

Go to your special place and find a comfortable position. Pick up a story, a Scripture text, something from which you believe you can learn. If it is a story or Scripture text, read it slowly. Now, breathing slowly, close your eyes. Picture the scene, the characters. Picture their clothes, the environment, their faces, as many details as you can. Smell the environment. If it is a scene with a meal, taste everything. Taste the food, the drink.

Let yourself feel. Feel the heat, the clothes, the textures. If it is a story, become a character in the scene. Don't just stand back as an observer. Stay with all the impressions. Let yourself feel what your character feels. Let yourself breathe slowly. Breathe in and out, slowly, deeply. Let yourself be with whatever impressions, insights, feelings, that come to you. When you feel ready, note in your journal some impressions or insights you received. Write any confusion or conflicts that may have surfaced. When you conclude this practice, be careful to be reverent with yourself. You may find that you would like to share something with your special companion. This is also fine to do.

5. Support Group

Strange as it may seem, I believe a support group is a definite practice to help you maintain a conscious contact with your God. It is a powerful thing to be with people who are sharing what is happening in their hearts and lives. When you sit with other people and listen to them share what is happening in their lives, you will be touched. No matter how different other people are from you, when they share how they are trying to work their program by walking these Steps, something gets "triggered" inside you.

This "heart connecting with heart" gives a lot of energy and hope. What remains is for you to then take the insight and work with it in your life.

Some prefer a set structure for their support-group meetings. Others prefer a more free-floating style. There are many ways to do this.

Some people prefer a group meeting where one of the Twelve Steps is read. After that, several people may want to share how they are experiencing a Step or their God or life.

Some people prefer a group where there is open discussion with a different leader each meeting. Sometimes a meeting "script" is written out, and sometimes there is nothing prepared.

Some people prefer a format where people speak to the group with short or long talks. These "speakers" share how their God is working in their life. Their talks are usually grouped into three parts: "What I was like," "What happened," and "What I am like now." It is really for each group of people to decide the style it most prefers or the combinations of styles.

Regardless of the style, however, in order to avoid the distractions of human interactions in groups, the literature and traditions from Alcoholics Anonymous repeatedly encourage its members to focus on "principles before personalities."[10] When the focus is the purpose of sharing one's experience, strength, and hope, instead of power struggles and group dynamics, then wonderful sharing can happen.

Leaders of meetings help to avoid chaos, but they lead as "trusted servants." They don't govern. All of the people who choose to be in a group are in charge, together.

These are discussions about a spiritual journey, and what is shared is received without comment. A sure way to sabotage a group is to allow personal sharing to turn into discussions. Discussions are in the head. Support groups are effective because each individual is heard with respect. It is not appropriate in this context to dominate and try to fix each other. You each keep eye contact. You nod supportively and minister to each other by sending caring love. You don't have to argue or defend yourself. Instead, you avoid what is called "cross talk." No comment is made upon what is said. You trust that the other person's Higher Power will touch his heart as you are being touched. It is not your job to do this. If, however, after checking out your motives with another, and with your God, you feel it is necessary to speak with someone, do so privately. Do this only after asking the person's permission first. Leave them free to decline your input too.

6. Treasure Board

A treasure board is a type of ongoing awareness raiser. To make a treasure board, take a piece of cardboard or a small bulletin board. Reflect upon the insights you gained from Steps One through Ten. Ask your God to help you and then select symbols or pictures or words that remind you of who you feel called to become. You can put up symbols of goals you would like to accomplish, ideals of virtues, anything you want. Pin them up.

Put your treasure board someplace where you will see it daily. Every few months, check your board. You will see some things that will have become realities. Others will remain in process. Praise and thank God and yourself for the completed gifts. Ask for help for the "not yets" that still remain on the treasure board. Take the others down so that there is always spiritual space in your life.

7. God Box

To make your God box, select a box that you like. Some people use a coffee can. Others use a cigar box. Others take a little wood box and decorate it in a very special manner.

Anytime you have a real concern, a problem, a worry, write it down on a little piece of paper. This can be a problem with a relationship, a fear, a financial need, a concern for the sickness of another. Put it into your God box, then let go of it, turning it over to the care of God as you understand him. You will be led to see what it is that you need to do.

Periodically, open your God box. You will be surprised how so many things that used to trouble you have already been taken care of.

8. Affirmations

Affirmations can sound very silly, but sometimes this method helps you open up to the possibilities extended to you in your newly found spiritual life. This strategy can be called *visualization* as well. It is a good strategy, but becomes a prayer when you ask God to touch your mind and heart. You let God tell you what to say. It is good to do this strategy with your special companion or with good friends so that you do not delude yourself. It can be very easy to "slip" into overinflation or underinflation of your opinion of yourself. Sharing your affirmations with your special companion can be a very precious opportunity for feedback and reassurance for you. Your special companion can also be a source of support and encouragement for you in another way. It is possible to affirm something in order to deepen in it when you already have it. It is also possible to "beat yourself up," affirming something you aren't ready for yet because more groundwork is necessary. Your special companion can help you to see which of these possibilities might be happening in your life.

The strategy is to reflect on a way of being or something you feel you are meant to do or a quality to become as in the treasure board strategy. Then you write a sentence affirming this quality in yourself, affirming the action of God in your life. You use the personal words "I" or "You" as you write your sentences. You use positive statements and present tense. You write results, abilities you want, using action and emotion words. You are very specific in what you write. Your sentences are balanced and realistic. They have to be at least halfway believable, or you will sabotage them yourself.

An example of an affirmation might be as follows:

I am a dynamic, energetic, compassionate woman. I serve my students, their parents, and the other teachers as each needs with love and enthusiasm.

I wrote this affirmation for myself at a time when I felt lethargic. My students were disturbed and dangerous. Money and resources were limited. Dysfunctional patterns were all over the place. It was easy to feel sour, frustrated, ineffective, and angry because I had an injured shoulder from an accident at school and felt trapped. I knew I had to "work on myself" before I could "be there" effectively for anyone else. In my heart I knew I needed to focus on recapturing my focus. This affirmation helped me. I read it once every morning and evening for a couple of weeks. I do my spiritual work, but it also helps sometimes to affirm that some other reality is possible.

9. Journaling

Some people are very faithful to their writing in the earlier Steps. You forget to continue this strategy as time goes on, however. A very powerful way for God to break through into your life is through this method of writing. It does not have to be complicated. Some people keep a spiral notebook and a pen near their bed. Others buy specially prepared books with fancy covers. The important thing is to pick up your book at the end of the day. Connect pen to paper, or fingers to the keyboard.

Some would say this is part of the Tenth Step, and this can be true. However, as you invite God to be with you, journaling is also a Step Eleven task. There is frequently a real communion and sense of peace experienced as you do this writing. This is not aggressive self-examination, but a more listening type of stance.

In your notebook, your journal, write anything that you want: ideas, feelings, secret desires. Share the love you have for your God. Express your gratitude for the life that is growing within you. If you have enjoyed a book, a poem, or a painting, write an insight you may have gained. The Spirit can be working deeply within you, and you come to see this as you write.

If you have a dream, write it down, and write what you think it means. Even if you are not formally schooled, God still finds a way to speak to your heart. God helps you understand what you need to know.

10. Mini-retreat on Your Death

This might seem morbid, but remembering that you will die is a good exercise. It helps you keep a perspective on things. One way to do this is to go away and re-treat your life with a new look. This can be an hour once a month, a day once a year, or whatever you feel is helpful.

One strategy is to be still and ponder the reality, then write your insights and the emotions that surfaced.

Another strategy is to draw three tombstones. One would say "Who I was." One would say "Who I am." One would say "Whom I'm invited to become." Figures 29, 30, and 31 offer samples of these three headstones. After drawing the tombstones, write a very honest letter to your God. If you need more paper, use it too. Write the words that surface. Use the first person, saying "I." Be sure to sign it. You will be surprised how moving this can be for you. You will see growth, encouragement, and challenge.

FIGURE 29

REFLECTION HEADSTONE
WHO I WAS...

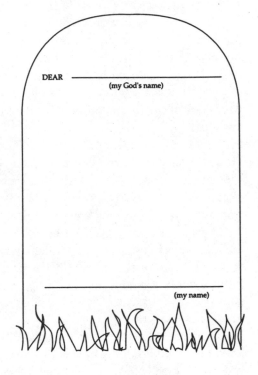

DEAR _____
(my God's name)

_____
(my name)

FIGURE 30

REFLECTION HEADSTONE
WHO I AM...

DEAR _____
(my God's name)

_____
(my name)

FIGURE 31

REFLECTION HEADSTONE
WHOM I AM INVITED
TO BECOME...

DEAR _____
(my God's name)

_____
(my name)

There are times when you can feel "blocked" when you try to journal or do a death reflection. You don't want to use words to do your "death meditation." Sometimes it is just as helpful to doodle or draw inside the tombstones. After this, be still and "ponder the work of your hands." Through crooked lines and color, God can still burst forth in your heart!

Eleventh Step Prayer

As with the other Steps, it is always helpful to place yourself in the presence of God through praying some words or by gesture to help yourself remember what you are about. A possible prayer to use is offered here.

God, (Or whatever name you wish to use to name your Higher Power), I thank you for leading me to a spiritual awakening. I ask you to help me keep my connection with you alive and vital in my life. Please keep me open and free from the confusion in my daily life. Through my prayers and meditation, I ask you for freedom from my self-will and from my old habits. Amen.

Twelve Steps Prayer

Sometimes a quick way to maintain a conscious contact, either first thing in the morning or during the day, is to pray a prayer that includes all of the Twelve Steps. A suggestion is offered below. You may wish to change it to say specifically the name of your Higher Power. You might also wish to write what it is that has been of concern for you in your life as your needs, your trap, your defects. Then write it out or type it as your own. Some people even get their prayer printed on special card stock and decorate it.

My God, I admit that without your help I am powerless in my life. It becomes unmanageable for me. I believe that you can restore me to wholeness and balance. I now turn my life and my will over to your care. I have made a searching and fearless moral inventory of myself. I have admitted to you, to myself, and to another person the exact nature of my wrongs. I am entirely ready to let you remove my remaining character defects. I ask you humbly, please remove my shortcomings, even those I do not yet see in myself. I have made direct amends to all the persons I have harmed, except when to do so would have injured them or others. I will continue to take my personal inventory, and when I am wrong, I will admit this promptly. I will seek through prayer and meditation to improve my conscious contact with you today. I pray only for knowledge of your will for me, and the power to carry it out. Please grant me the grace to carry the message of your love and care to others. Help me to practice the principles of these Twelve Steps in all my affairs. Amen.

And now, as you continue taking all of these Steps, including Steps Ten and Eleven, you begin to practice Step Twelve. It can be very easy to want to rest now, to bask in your newly found "spiritual awakening." If you do, though, you will not continue the journey. That's part of life. If you have a gift and you do not give it away, you lose it. Like a body of water, if there is no outflow and new inflow, it becomes stagnant. To avoid "slipping," Twelve Step living is essential. We have to "pass it on." This is discussed more in Part Four.

Notes

[1] Alcoholics Anonymous, *Alcoholics Anonymous 3rd ed.* (New York: Alcoholics Anonymous World Services, Inc., 1976). Chapter 5.

[2] David Daniels, M.D. Professional Training Seminar, Vallambrosa Retreat Center, August 1992.

[3] Alcoholics Anonymous. *Alcoholics Anonymous,* 3rd ed., Chapter 5.

[4] *Ibid,* 76.

[5] Alcoholics Anonymous, *As Bill Sees It* (New York: Alcoholics Anonymous World Services, Inc., 1967).

[6] Alcoholics Anonymous. *Alcoholics Anonymous,* 3rd ed., 164.

[7] *Ibid.,* 136.

[8]Helen Palmer, *The Enneagram: Understanding Yourself and the Others in Your Life* (San Francisco: Harper & Row, 1988).

[9]Bernie Siegel, *Peace, Love and Healing: Body, Mind Communication, the Path to Self Healing and Exploration* (San Francisco: Harper Collins, 1990).

[10]Alcoholics Anonymous, *Twelve Steps and Twelve Traditions* (New York: Alcoholics Anonymous World Services, Inc., 1981), 187, 192.

PART 4

Continuing With the Enneagram

Chapter 14

Step Twelve:
Carry the Message to Others

Step Twelve: "Having had a spiritual awakening as the result of these Steps, we tried to carry this message to [others], and to practice these principles in all our affairs."

You have received a free gift through these Twelve Steps. There are many ways you can respond to this gift.

There are some individuals who take this new found level of "relief" and hold on to it. They know that they have found God. They know that their God is real for them. Some are content as long as their compulsions are not making them miserable. They don't go any further than their own good feeling of new life. They don't help to serve others or practice the Twelve Steps in their lives. This is not practicing the Twelfth Step.

Other people work the first Eleven Steps for a while. They become comfortable with themselves and with their God, and they try to live their lives as good people. This is better, but it is still not practicing the Twelfth Step.

Other people seem to flourish with the Twelve Step journey, and they try to practice the principles in all their affairs. However, these people can also tend to go "hog wild" with their zeal to share this message with others. Instead of serving others, they are compulsively meeting their own needs by imposing upon others. They wear people out imposing their perceptions, their judgments of what the others need to do to be whole.

They forget the principle that our work is to detach with love, to "let go and let God." They are "off the mark" in this aspect of the Twelve Steps. They forget to share gently and respectfully and then to stop. People may not be progressing as you feel they need to do, but this is not your responsibility. You are not their God. Those who act as if they are someone else's God miss out on opportunities to practice Step Twelve.

To continue flourishing in the Twelve Step spirituality, you will find that it is necessary to share with others the good news of your life. If you do not do so, you may find that you "slip" and return to your old ways. If you practice your Steps faithfully, you will also experience a life that feels as if it is new. It feels new and fulfilling for you when you are able to help and serve others freely as people really need. You will find that you want to reach out respectfully in love to those who seem to need what you are able to offer. You are also finding a new peace and enjoyment in your life at home, at work, and in your relationships.

This is practicing the Twelfth Step. All of your character defects are constantly challenged by the gift of your new God-relationship. Those of you living the practice of the Twelve Steps find yourself driven to live "right attitudes." You find a drive to be "God attitudes," to live by God's principles in your affairs. You find a hunger to be, as the Scriptures say, the beatitudes (the "be-attitudes") alive.

Considerations in Practicing Step Twelve

Here are some helps to continue to take Step Twelve.

1. New Glasses Method

There is nothing as frustrating as feeling you are doing well and then "wham!"—a challenge comes into a your life to throw you off your path. You have made a personal investment to walk a Twelve Step path, to observe your character, your defects and assets, and to let God work in and through you. Inevitably, some event, some person, some happening, shows up to turn you upside down and push you to really have to "practice these principles in all your affairs." If you don't, you'll be right back at your starting point.

At these times it is advisable to act as if you are seeing with a whole new eyeglass prescription. Put on a brand-new pair of inner glasses and let yourself see everything in life as an opportunity to practice your program. The next part is to practice, practice, practice! Do your Twelve Steps all the time. Where you err, see it and make your amends. Where you have pain, fear, rage, resentment, share this with your special companion or with someone else. Talk does wonderful things. By all means, take stock of yourself, and give God time too. All will fall into place.

2. Carry This Message to Others

Our society needs people who know and love their God, no matter who or what they call God. Our society needs people fully alive, loving, and ready to share their experience, and by doing this, to touch others with their hope and with their love.

I would offer a caution here. It is very important to be careful, to exercise caution in your practice of sharing the good news of what God has done in your life. The underlying principle of this Step is that it is you who are the real "instrument of God." The Enneagram and the Twelve Steps are methods. But you are not God. You are God's tool. It is people, sharing, risking, relating, that let the goodness of God come alive for others. Our world needs changing, and it is each of us, touching each other, who lets the change happen. Be gentle. Be respectful, Be real.

3. Gather With Others

I hesitate to say, "join a group." This can trigger a negative image for many. It can bring up feelings that will lead you to say, "I'm busy," "I'm doing fine," "I don't need an Enneagram group, a Twelve Step group, or a spiritual support group." If you are open to some sharing with others, you will be led to find the connection that you are meant to find. Don't worry about it. You will find some way to share with others, as you need. It is not important what the connection is called. Just stay open.

Some individuals who are trying to grow begin Twelve Step sharing groups in their parishes. This is a beautiful service because it allows individuals to share what is going on in their lives with each other. A safe, supportive environment becomes available for anyone who comes. It doesn't matter that perhaps some of what is shared is dark and difficult for some who come on any given night.

Some of you could form support group of people who are interested in the Enneagram or a particular Enneagram Point, to share what is going on for you in your life and growth. You would find encouragement and support for yourself while offering support to the others.

Some people have set up Bible groups. These groups are not only study groups, though this may be part of it. The groups are for sharing how the Word is coming alive in their lives. People share their struggles and receive the struggles of others both reverently and supportively.

Another concept I have seen used is the faith-sharing group. This group is open to anyone who wants to participate from a work location, a neighborhood, or a specific church family.

Groups already exist that are said to be based on spirituality. These include church groups, Bible groups, religious communities, and so forth. These groups provide continuous support with a level of faith sharing that renews all its members.

Depending upon each one's need, these groups can be male, female, or mixed.

I would offer a word of encouragement here. The time may come when you do not feel like going to a meeting of a group. You will be tired, busy, or bored. It is at these times that a level of commitment is required. You need to know your motivation and be willing to "be there" for others too. This is when Step Twelve comes in. If you are "working your program," you are alive and life-filled. Others will want what you have, but they won't see it if you aren't willing to be there for them. This is called *fellowship*. Some call it family. Some call it community. Ongoing growth is made much easier when you have this resource in your life. Your task is to be there for others.

3. Open Up to Your World

When you are working Steps One through Eleven and are trying to practice Step Twelve, you can still remain in a state of delusion that can be very comfortable. I am not advocating that it is good to be uncomfortable, but it is important to stay open to your God in your heart. When you are humble and open, new truths will always present themselves for you. More is always being revealed.

What Step Twelve challenges you to do is to practice these principles in all your affairs. It is good to practice them at home, at work, at church, at school, and at your clubs and groupings, but you are all part of broader groupings, as you will eventually discover. For many of you, this is a new thing, to think of spirituality in a way that is so much broader than you knew before. For example, LaChance suggests that we use the Twelve Steps to look at our ecological spirituality. In his book *Greenspirit*, he suggests that we are all addicted to overconsuming and polluting ourselves and our environment to the edge of oblivion. He suggests that the solution is not in theology, but in a new conversion, a new spirituality of connecting with our environment called Ecological Spirituality.[1] Rohr, Crosby, Fox, and Elgin all invite us to look at our lives, our fears, our emotional needs in relation to peoples of all colors and cultures.

You are "part of" a town, a city, a state, a country, and a global community. Perhaps there are affairs you need to look at regarding your participation in these areas. If so, your Higher Power will lead you to know this, as well, if you remain with "eyes to see and the ears to hear."

Twelfth Step Prayer

As with each Step, it is good to begin with a prayer. This could be prayed every morning or several times during the day. If the words are not your preference, speak from your own heart or use a gesture to express your desire to serve others and to practice these principles as your God would lead you to do.

A sample Twelfth Step Prayer is included here.

_____(Name your Higher Power, your God), thank you for my spiritual awakening. Help me pass it on to the people I meet in all the situations of my life, sensitively and as they need. Help me to walk day by day, step by step, on the road of spiritual progress. Help me to practice the principles of this life in all I do and say. Amen.

Notes

[1] LaChance, Albert, *Greenspirit: Twelve Steps in Ecological Spirituality* (Rockport, MA: Element Books, 1991). Also see an interview with LaChance in "Planet in Recovery," *Yoga Journal*, Nov./Dec. 1992, 71-75, 125-126.

PART 5

Concluding
Thoughts

If you have read this book thoroughly, you might feel ready and eager to "jump in" and to begin to work these steps, moving from your fixation on to greater ways of being. Before you begin to work these Twelve Steps, I offer a few closing thoughts for your consideration.

On Two Steppers

It is a very easy to fall into a trap called a *Two Stepper*. For this individual the level of sincerity is true and real, but a tricky delusion can set in. There is an incredibly powerful peace that can come from really taking Step One honestly. You will know an outrageously real sense of "awe" when you finally observe your real self as you are in your Enneagram Point with your fixation in "living color." Your experience of realization can be so real, like a "slap across the face," that you will know how deluded you have been and how powerless you have become.

So powerful is the peace that can come from really taking Step One honestly that you can feel you are already recovering. When you were so disgusted with your patterns, you knew you desperately needed help and you screamed at God, "All right, I give up! Help!"

That cry of anguish is so deeply based and all-consuming that it can lead you to believe you have quickly taken Steps Two and Three. The trap is that the personal belief in a God is not yet there. The willingness to let God do it with you was really present. The really serious decision to do whatever it would take was not made.

After having this powerful release experienced in Step One, some individuals can then jump right into spreading their "good news" and even shoving it down others' throats. This can be done through the use of a feeling of a superior position because they have not yet experienced the powerful life-giving thrill of humility blooming in their lives. They have not known personally the peace of the Twelve Steps. This is a peace that is better than any understanding in the human mind, but it must be purchased by "walking a walk," not only by "talking the talk." The journey of the Twelve Steps and the Enneagram is not only in the head, but in the head, the heart, the gut, the total human being with fixations, defects, instinctual ways of operating, and higher gifts.

If you have the experience of being around those who are just beginning this Twelve Step path, please be patient with them. It is a good service that you do, to be willing to listen to others share about their life. It is healthy for people who are new to anything to want to share, and even to wear the listener out with their sharing. In AA they call these people *newcomers*, and it is a fragile, sensitive time for them. In religious life these people are called *novices*. In the Catholic Church they are called *catechumens*. The experience is the same for all people new to something. It takes love to listen! It doesn't matter if this is a job, a marriage, a Twelve Step program, an exercise routine, a diet program. Please do not judge that newcomers are Two Stepping.

Keep an eye on yourself and walk your own path. If you think you might be Two Stepping, get yourself a special companion and start again.

On Five Steppers

People who are Five Steppers are also sincere. They have taken Steps One, Two, and Three. They have really begun to pray, to meditate, to read, to focus. They recommit their life to God continually. They do "let go and let God." They let themselves remember the maxim "Easy does it." They pray. They practice Step Eleven. They also try to practice the principles of the Twelve Steps in all of their affairs. They work very hard to do all this too!

Unfortunately, they can be very deluded if they walk the Twelve Step path this way. As I listed in the Introduction, there are three parts of the Twelve Steps. They are:

1. To trust God (Steps One, Two, Three)
2. To clean the inner house (Steps Four through Eleven)
3. To help others (Step Twelve)

A Five Stepper forgets about Steps Four through Ten. He or she forgets to take out the garbage and scrub out the deeply ground-in dirt. If I may use an analogy, the Five Steppers have made themselves a sandwich, but have only used bread. They have left out the essential fillers, the protein source and vegetables, the inner tissue builders of their lives. The outer bread can be excellent and nutritious, but it is not enough for a spiritual journey. Five Steppers have forgotten to chew on the roughage that cleans out the toxins that stay inside.

Eventually, others will see Five Steppers as what AA-ers refer to as "dry drunks." Life for Five Steppers can be very hard. They have tried, sincerely tried, to cast out one demon, but seven others slipped in its place. Five Stepping can be much harder than taking all the Twelve Steps because the promised, spiritual experience continues to elude these individuals. They are "doing" the work, "doing" their prayers, rather than opening up to a lifetime of wonderful surprises as they "become the walk." They miss out on true service too. Because they have never quite experienced the "spiritual revolution," they are never quite able to become "a program of attraction" for others as fully as they could. They can teach and preach their understanding of the "good news," but something still doesn't "compute" for the listener.

On Humility, Not Humiliation

This program requires rigorous honesty. It requires openness and willingness to be humble. It is easy to fear the Twelve Steps as a path or the Enneagram insights because you fear you will be required to be humiliated. Nobody wants humiliation. It would be sick to want to be subservient and humiliated. You are trying to move beyond sickness, not into it!

A rule of thumb is to take no Step until three criteria are present. 1.) You have dialogued with your special companion, and you both agree you are ready for the next Step. 2.) You have listened to your own heart and mind and gut, and you feel ready to move on. 3.) You believe deeply that your God is inviting you to move on.

If any of the three criteria is missing, you might consider this very seriously. Perhaps you need a different special companion. Perhaps you need to listen better to your special companion. Perhaps you are being cowardly, and you are ready to leap into the next Step, even if you have doubts.

On Your Special Companion

As you progress on your Twelve Step journey, share what is happening with your special companion. You have picked this person because you know this person loves you as you are, so be at peace. Most of us are not accustomed to sharing with someone on a regular basis. Yet, this is a gift of intimacy that is a basic human need.

Regardless of your state in life, you are entitled to this. It is a privilege to have someone to help you through your darkness and pain. It is a privilege to have someone there for you, to encourage you to grow in all the areas of your life. If people accept your invitation, do not hesitate to really use them. Draw upon them.

Despite all the encouragement to use spiritual directors, many of us do not know how to share what is going on in our lives with another person. This confusion exists for a variety of reasons. Some people wonder what there is to talk about with another person on a regular basis. Some have problems finding a person they feel they can trust. Some people choose to use a confessor, but they focus on a specific act of confessing sin only, instead of developing skills to lead to a "spiritual revolution." Some use spiritual directors but restrict the conversations to the areas of the spiritual domain of life without focusing on all the other related areas that affect us, such as the emotions or the physical, social and work worlds.

When you pick someone to trust as a special companion, you are opening up to a wonderful world of life, growth, and change. It is a powerful gift to share anything with someone and to know the person will still love you. Sometimes there is so much more to share—your feelings, behavior, fears, anger, frustration, little triumphs, and defeats. For those of you on the Twelve Step journey, this has been found to be very true. It is so much easier to walk these Steps if you share your reflection with at least one other person.

The qualification for being someone's companion is that you are also working these Steps and sharing honestly of yourself with someone. No advanced degree is required because it is humility found in a relationship with God that you are really seeking. You will be led to see the person with whom you will feel comfortable. This person can be male or female, priest, religious, or layperson.

What is important for you is that your special companion understands what you are wanting to do, and that this person is willing to be with you when you call upon him or her.

It is also an honor and a privilege to be invited to serve another person as a special companion. If you are asked and if you feel unworthy, trust God. You will find your own progress increasing as you walk with another on the spiritual path. This is a special, special opportunity to be embraced with a gentle spirit of humility and reverence. The person asked you for a reason. Unless you are overextending yourself already, please consider very seriously before you decline someone's request. This is a real Twelfth Step service.

Sometimes it is good to have a companion of the same sex just because of the intimate nature of details that you might share and the attraction that can result. In the Twelve Step literature, though, this is only a suggestion. The principle is that each of us is trusted to listen to our own heart and to do as we feel God is guiding us. If the person you most feel you "connect" with for your sharing is of the opposite sex, then it is all right to try this. Just be open to admitting that it is not working for you, if you sense a need to look for another person as a companion.

The criteria to use to ask someone to serve as your special companion is that you feel this person cares for you, has common sense, and is also "walking the spiritual walk." As they say in AA, this person is also "working his own program."

Your companion agrees to invite you to honesty when necessary. This person is ready and eager to celebrate your growth with you. As you grow, you may find yourself broadening and using many others to share your journey in addition to the special companion. In your Twelve Step/ Enneagram journey you will find that much more will be revealed to you of ways to grow, to change, to deepen. Habits have been a long time becoming ingrained. You may need to heal the body even at a cellular level. You may need to heal from disease of the body and the mind.

You might need to use physicians, a psychologist, a spiritual support group, the people with whom you live, other friends, your superiors, your employer, or a confessor to help you with specific areas in which you need to grow. Each individual is like an onion with the layers peeling off slowly at the hand of a very gentle God.

With all this help, though, it is very important to keep your focus on the role of your special companion for you so that confusion of roles does not occur.

If you find others who try to judge the quality of your walk, or if they try to dominate you, let go of them inside your own heart. Work Steps One, Two, and Three on this matter. Let go of their importance to you. Some people might try to suggest what to put into your inventory or how to "work your program." Even if they are right or have much more experience than you, if you do not want to give them permission to intrude, you don't have to. It may also be that they are wrong in their judgments about you. You do not have to explain yourself to them.

Remember that you have your own needs, and anyone judging you is working out of his or her own compulsion. Remember that all people are "fellow suffering human beings," with their own delusion, their own ways of "paying attention," of perceiving reality. Though it can be hard to do at the time, it is important to stand back and not judge each other. The invitation is to live the Twelfth Step with compassion and humility. Even if it is very hard, the challenge is to do as the book *Alcoholics Anonymous* suggests. For our own sake, we need to pray for them, and resentments and hurts will fall away.[1] Ironically, we all end up even more healed and whole!

On the K.I.S.S. Method (Keep It Simple, Stupid!)

The last suggestion I would offer is one that was given to those in Alcoholics Anonymous in 1950. It was offered by Dr. Bob, one of the cofounders of AA, in an address at their First International Convention in Cleveland, Ohio. He said:

There are two or three things that flashed into my mind on which it would be fitting to lay a little emphasis. One is the simplicity of our program. Let's not louse it all up with Freudian complexes and things that are interesting to the scientific mind, but have very little to do with our actual...work. Our Twelve

Steps, when simmered down to the last, resolve themselves into the words "love" and "service." You understand what love is, and you understand what service is. So let's bear those two things in mind.[2]

If *Overcoming Your Compulsions* has helped anyone to love and serve even a little better, I thank God. Pass it on.

On Learning More

There are several ways to keep growing in the Twelve Steps and the Enneagram. You can observe yourself and how you live. You can share with others and listen to them using your special companion and a support/sharing group. You can look for good teachers and use them. You can also study the Twelve Steps and the Enneagram with good teachers.

To learn more about the Twelve Steps, you can go to workshops and Twelve Step meetings as a visitor (or as a participant). To learn more about the Enneagram, you can look at the authors listed in the Resources section (Appendix 1). Many of these authors give workshops and training sessions. If you contact them, they will let you know what is available for you. Many also publish a list of teachers whom they would recommend as able to teach the Enneagram in your area. Retreat centers and churches are becoming more aware of the value of the Enneagram and the Twelve Steps for growth. If they are not offering opportunities, they often do have resources they can recommend.

Notes

[1] AA literature, *Seventh Step Praying for Others*.

[2] Alcoholics Anonymous, *Pass It On* (New York, NY: Alcoholics Anonymous World Services, Inc., 1984).

PART 6

Appendices

Appendix 1

Resources

Alcoholics Anonymous. *Alcoholics Anonymous (3rd Edition)*. New York. NY: Alcoholics Anonymous World Services Inc., 1976.

Alcoholics Anonymous. *Alcoholics Anonymous Comes of Age*. New York, NY: Alcoholics Anonymous World Services, Inc., 1957.

Alcoholics Anonymous. *As Bill Sees It*. New York, NY: Alcoholic Anonymous World Services, Inc., 1967.

Alcoholics Anonymous. *Pass It On: The Story of Bill Wilson and How the A.A. Message Reached the World*. New York, NY: Alcoholics Anonymous World Services, Inc., 1984.

Alcoholics Anonymous. *Twelve Steps and Twelve Traditions*. New York, NY: Alcoholics Anonymous World Services, Inc., 1981.

Alcoholics Anonymous. *Where Does It Say So?* New York, NY: Alcoholics Anonymous World Services, Inc., 1976.

Anthony, Edd. *Reflections on the Serenity Prayer*. Audiotape. Victorville: Franciscan Canticle, Inc., 1992.

Beesing, Maria, Robert J. Nogosek, and Patrick H. O'Leary. *The Enneagram: A Journey of Self Discovery*. Denville, NJ: Dimension Books, 1984.

"C," Chuck. *A New Pair of Glasses*. Irvine: New Look Publishing Co., 1984.

Cogan, Susan, "Your God," *Intercom*. International Newsletter of the English Province of the Daughters of Mary and Joseph. 55 Fitzjames Ave. Croydon, Surrey, England. CRO 5DN.

Elgin, Duane. *Voluntary Simplicity: Toward a Way of Life That Is Outwardly Simple, Inwardly Rich*. New York, NY: William Morrow, Inc., 1981.

Goldberg, Michael. "Inside the Enneagram Wars." *L.A... Weekly*, October 15-21, 1993, 16-26.

Hart, Thomas. *The Art of Christian Listening*. Mahwah, NJ: Paulist Press, 1981.

Henry, Kathleen. *The Book of Enneagram Prayers*. Jamaica Plain, MA: Alabaster Jar Liturgical Arts, 1987.

Hurley, Kathleen and Theodore Dobson. *What's My Type? Use the Enneagram System of Nine Personality Types to Discover Your Best Self*. San Francisco, CA: HarperSF, 1991.

Kelsey, Morton. *Companions on the Inner Way: The Art of Spiritual Guidance*. New York, NY: Crossroad Publishing, 1985.

Keyes, Margaret Frings. *Emotions and the Enneagram: Working Through Your Shadow Life Script*. Muir Beach, CA: Molysdatur Publications, 1990.

Keyes, Margaret Frings. *The Enneagram Relationship Workbook: A Self and Partnership Assessment Guide*. Muir Beach, CA: Molysdatur Publications, 1992.

Naranjo, Claudio. *Ennea-Type Structures: Self-Analysis for the Seeker*. Nevada City, CA: Gateways Book & Tapes, 1990.

National Council of Churches of Christ in U.S.A. *New Revised Standard Version Bible*, Grandville, MI: World Bible Publishers, 1989.

Palmer, Helen. *The Enneagram: Understanding Yourself and the Others in Your Life*. San Francisco, CA: Harper SF, 1991.

Poe, Steven E., and Frances E Poe. *A Concordance to Alcoholics Anonymous*. Carson City: Purple Salamander Press, 1990.

Peck, M. Scott. *People of the Lie: The Hope for Healing Human Evil*. New York, NY: Touchstone Books, 1985.

Riso, Don Richard. *Personality Types: Using the Enneagram for Self-Discovery*. Boston, MA: Houghton Mifflin Co., 1987.

Riso, Don Richard. *Understanding the Enneagram: The Practical Guide to Personality Types*. Boston MA: Houghton Mifflin Co., 1990.

Roget & Day, A. Colin. *Roget's International Thesaurus of the Bible*. San Francisco, CA: HarperCollins, 1992.

Rohr, Richard and Andreas Ebert. *Discovering the Enneagram: An Ancient Tool for a New Spiritual Journey*. New York, NY: Crossroad, 1990.

Rohr, Richard, Andreas Ebert and Others. *Experiencing the Enneagram*. New York, NY: Crossroad Publishing Co., 1992.

Sellner, Edward. *Mentoring: The Ministry of Spiritual Kinship*. Notre Dame, IN: Ave Maria Press, 1990.

Siegel, Bernie. *Peace, Love and Healing: Bodymind Communication and the Path to Self-Healing: an Exploration*. San Francisco, CA: HarperCollins, 1990.

Speeth, Kathleen. *The Gurdjieff Work*. Los Angeles, CA: J.P. Tarcher, Inc., 1989.

Tickerhoff, Bernard. *Conversion & the Enneagram: Transformation of the Self in Christ*. Denville, NJ: Dimension Books, Inc., 1991.

Trungpa, Chogyam. *Cutting Through Spiritual Materialism*. Boston, MA: Shambala Publications, Inc., 1987.

Zuercher, Suzanne. *Enneagram Companions: Growing in Relationships and Spiritual Direction*. Notre Dame, IN: Ave Maria Press, 1993.

Zuercher, Suzanne. *Enneagram Spirituality: from Compulsion to Contemplation*. Notre Dame, IN: Ave Maria Press, 1992.

Appendix 2

Alcoholics Anonymous Sources and the Twelve Steps[1]

Key Words	Source	Pages
AA Mottoes	AA	135
AA Mottoes	AA	550
AA Mottoes	Bill Sees	11
AA Mottoes	12 /12	153
AA Mottoes	Bill Sees	11
Acceptance	AA	449
All Steps (Problem /Solution)	AA	12–13
All Steps	AA	59
Allergy	AA	xxiv
Belief (20 expressions)	AA	xxi
Belief	AA	12
Belief	AA	25
Belief	AA	28
Belief	AA	46–49
Belief	AA	62
Belief	AA	68
Belief	AA	93
Belief	12 /12	26–28
Companion	AA	18
Companion	AA	72–73
Companion	AA	89
Companion	AA	90–95
Companion	AA	121
Companion	AA	177–178
Companion	AA Comes of Age	10
Companion	Bill Sees	165
Companion	Bill Sees	102
Companion	Bill Sees	212
Companion	12 /12	60–61
Companion	12 /12	133

Key Words	Source	Pages
Faith	12 /12	145
Faith	AA	16
Easy Does It	AA	135
First Things First	AA	135
Goal: Share Experience, Strength, and Hope	AA	xxii
God	AA	xvi
God	AA	12–14
God	AA	28
God	AA	45–47
God	AA	51–52
God	AA	60–62
God	AA	67–68
God	AA	85–86
God	AA	98–100
God	AA	120–124
Helping Others: Avocation	AA	xiii
H.O.W. We Recover	AA	xiii
(Honest, Open, Willing)	AA	550
H.O.W.	AA	570
Humility	12 /12	30
Humility	12 /12	46
Humility	12 /12	59–60
Humility	12 /12	71–76
Humility	Bill Sees	44
Joy of Living	AA	15
Keep It Simple	AA Conference 7 /3 /50	
Let Go, Let God!	AA	58
Live and Let Live	AA	135
Membership Requirement	AA	xiv
Moral Inventory	AA	xvi
More Will Be Revealed	AA	164
One Day at a Time	Bill Sees	11
Principles Before Personalities	12 /12	192
Professionals: Use Them	AA	134
Progress, Not Perfection	AA	60
Progress, Not Perfection	Bill Sees	44
Promises	AA	8
Promises	AA	63
Promises	AA	83–84

Key Words	Source	Pages
Promises	AA	115
Promises	AA	152
Psyche Plus Body	AA	xxiv
Religion	AA	11
Religion	AA	49
Religion	AA	62
Religion	AA	74
Religion	AA	87
Religion	AA	90
Religion	AA	93
Religion	AA	132
Roles for God	AA	62
Self-Centeredness	AA	14
Serenity	AA	152
Serenity Prayer	Bill Sees	20
Serenity Prayer	Bill Sees	108
Serenity Prayer	AA Comes Age	196
Solution	AA	25
Spiritual Awakening	AA Comes Age	13
Spiritual Awakening	Bill Sees	8
Spiritual Awakening	Bill Sees	85
Spiritual Awakening	Bill Sees	152
Spiritual Awakening	Bill Sees	171
Spiritual Awakening	12 /12	110
Spiritual Awakening	12 /12	112
Spiritual Experience	AA	8
Spiritual Experience	AA	25–27
Spiritual Experience	AA	75
Spiritual Experience	AA	84–85
Spiritual Experience	AA	130
Spiritual Experience	AA	569–570
Spiritual Experience	Bill Sees	178
Spiritual Experience	Bill Sees	217
Spiritual Experience	Bill Sees	242–246
Spiritual Experience	Bill Sees	281
Spiritual Message	AA	12
Spiritual Progress	AA	60
Spiritual Progress, Not Spiritual Perfection	Bill Sees	44
Step One (Unmanageable)	AA	8

Key Words	Source	Pages
Step One	AA	25
Step One	AA	30–35
Step One	AA	60
Step One	12/12	21–24
Step Two (Came to Believe)	AA	9
Step Two	AA	25
Step Two	AA	44–57
Step Two	12/12	25–33
Step Three (Decide)	AA	60–63
Step Three	12/12	34–41
Step Four (Inventory)	AA	18
Step Four	AA	71
Step Four	AA	63–71
Step Four	AA	145
Step Four	AA	151–152
Step Four	12/12	42–54
Step Five (Admit)	AA	72–75
Step Five	Bill Sees	165
Step Five	12/12	55-62
Step Six (Become Ready)	AA	76
Step Six	12/12	63–69
Step Seven (Ask)	AA	76
Step Seven	12/12	70–76
Step Eight (List Amends)	AA	76
Step Eight	12/12	77–82
Step Nine (Make Amends)	AA	76–83
Step Nine	12/12	83–87
Step Ten (Maintain)	AA	84–85
Step Ten	12/12	88–95
Step Eleven (Conscious Contact)	AA	85-88
Step Eleven	12/12	96–105
Step Twelve (Live Right, Serve)	AA	12
Step Twelve	AA	89–105
Step Twelve	12/12	106-125
Trigger Cycle	AA	xxvi
Trust God, Clean House	AA	98
Twelve Traditions	AA	xix
Twelve Traditions	AA	564
Types of Alcoholics (Five)	AA	xxviii
Worship: Return to Places of	12/12	98

The Twelve Steps
As Written by Alcoholics Anonymous[2]

1. We admitted we were powerless over alcohol—that our lives had become unmanageable.
2. Came to believe that a Power greater than ourselves could restore us to sanity.
3. Made a decision to turn our will and our lives over to the care of God as we understood Him.
4. Made a searching and fearless moral inventory of ourselves.
5. Admitted to God, to ourselves, and to another human being the exact nature of our wrongs.
6. Were entirely ready to have God remove all these defects of character.
7. Humbly asked Him to remove our shortcomings.
8. Made a list of all persons we had harmed, and became willing to make amends to them all.
9. Made direct amends to such people wherever possible, except when to do so would injure them or others.
10. Continued to take personal inventory and when we were wrong promptly admitted it.
11. Sought through prayer and meditation to improve our conscious contact with God as we understood Him, praying only for knowledge of His will for us and the power to carry that out.
12. Having had a spiritual awakening as the result of these Steps, we tried to carry this message to alcoholics, and to practice these principles in all our affairs.

Appendix 3

Scriptures Used in Appendices

The books of the Bible cited in Appendices are listed here. They are listed in the order of their appearance in the Bible.

Books of the Bible Selected

Old Testament	New Testament
Exodus	Matthew
Leviticus	Mark
Numbers	Luke
Deuteronomy	John
Joshua	Acts
1 Samuel	Romans
2 Samuel	1 Corinthians
1 Kings	2 Corinthians
2 Kings	Galatians
1 Chronicles	Ephesians
2 Chronicles	Philippians
Nehemiah	Colossians
Job	1 Thessalonians
Psalms	2 Thessalonians
Proverbs	1 Timothy
Ecclesiastes	2 Timothy
Song of Songs	Titus

Old Testament	New Testament
Isaiah	Hebrews
Jeremiah	James
Lamentations	1 Peter
Ezekiel	2 Peter
Daniel	1 John
Hosea	Revelation
Micah	
Habakkuk	
Zechariah	

Appendix 4

Scriptures and the Twelve Steps

These Scripture references are offered for your prayer and reflection with the Twelve Steps. Scripture references are listed in each appendix as they appear in the Bible unless they are clustered together with a specific phrase. The verses are summarized below the reference to help the reader. The references cited are only a few of the many that could have been selected. If you wish to find more references, help to do this can be found in the following sources: the Bible; a concordance of the Bible that lists words actually used in the Bible; a biblical dictionary of the Bible; *Roget's International Thesaurus of the Bible*.

Step One: Surrender

Joshua 22:16
Are you turning away from the Lord?
What is this treachery that you have committed against the God of Israel in turning away today from following the LORD, by building yourselves an altar today in rebellion against the LORD?

2 Samuel 12:12
Give up doing things in secret.
For you did it secretly; but I will do this thing before all Israel, and before the sun.

Psalm 6:2–7
If you are really tired and weak, the Lord can heal you.
v.2. Be gracious to me, O LORD, *for I am languishing; / O* LORD, *heal me, for my bones are shaking with terror.*
v.3. My soul also is struck with terror, / while you, O LORD—*how long?*
v.4. Turn, O LORD, *save my life; / deliver me for the sake of your steadfast love.*
v.6. I am weary with my moaning; / every night I flood my bed with tears; / I drench my couch with my weeping.
v.7. My eyes waste away because of grief; / they grow weak because of all my foes.

Psalm 18:6
In your distress call on the Lord.
In my distress I called upon the LORD; / *to my God I cried for help… / He heard my voice.*

Psalm 30:10
Ask the Lord to hear you, He will do so.
Hear, O LORD, *and be gracious to me! / O* LORD, *be my helper!*

Psalm 31:9
If you are in trouble, God will help you.
Be gracious to me, O LORD, *for I am in distress; / my eye wastes away from grief, / my soul and body also.*

Psalm 38:3
God can heal you if you are sick.
There is no soundness in my flesh because of your indignation; / there is no health in my bones because of my sin.

Psalm 44:15
Tell God if you are ashamed.
All day long my disgrace is before me, / and shame has covered my face.

Psalm 69:1–3
Someone can help you.
v.1. Save me, O God, / for the waters have come up to my neck.
v.2. I sink in deep mire, / where there is no foothold; / I have come into deep

waters, / and the flood sweeps over me.
v.3. I am weary with my crying; / my throat is parched. / My eyes grow dim / with waiting for my God.

Psalm 88:1–4
Cry out. He will hear your cry.
v.1. O LORD, God of my salvation, / when, at night, I cry out in your presence.
v.2. Let my prayer come before you; / incline your ear to my cry.
v.3. For my soul is full of troubles, / and my life draws near to Sheol.
v.4. I am counted among those who go down to the Pit; / I am like those who have no help.

Proverbs 21:2
You are deluded, fooled that your way is right in your own eyes.
All deeds are right in the sight of the doer, / but the LORD weighs the heart.

Isaiah 30:11
You turn away from the path, and stop trying to listen.
Leave the way, turn aside from the path, / let us hear no more about the Holy One of Israel.

Jeremiah 3:3
You don't have the sensitivity to feel shame about how you act.
Therefore the showers have been withheld, / and the spring rain has not come; / yet you have the forehead of a whore, / you refuse to be ashamed.

Jeremiah 5:21
You just don't see or hear the way you really are.
[This people have eyes, but do not see.] Hear this, O foolish and senseless people, / who have eyes, but do not see, / who have ears, but do not hear.

Jeremiah 6:15
You don't have the sensitivity to feel shame about how you act.
They acted shamefully, they committed abomination; / yet they were not ashamed, / they did not know how to blush. / Therefore they shall fall among those who fall; / at the time that I punish them, / they shall be overthrown, says the LORD.

Jeremiah 10:23
You are not really as much in charge as you think.
I know, O LORD, that the way of human beings is not in their control, / that mortals as they walk cannot direct their steps.

Jeremiah 25:5
Turn from your evil way.
When they said, "Turn now, everyone of you, from your evil way and wicked doings, and you will remain upon the land that the LORD has given to you and your ancestors from of old and forever."

Ezekiel 12:2
You just don't see or hear the truth.
Mortal, you are living in the midst of a rebellious house, who have eyes to see but do not see, who have ears to hear but do not hear.

Matthew 7:16
Be real, because your fruits come from who you are.
You will know them by their fruits. Are grapes gathered from thorns, or figs from thistles?

Matthew 9:13
God is calling you to admit your needs.
Go and learn what this means, "I desire mercy, not sacrifice." For I have come to call not the righteous but sinners.

Matthew 11:20
Jesus scolds people for not repenting and "turning their lives around."
Then he began to reproach the cities in which most of his deeds of power had been done, because they did not repent.

Matthew 13:15
You are responsible to open your eyes and to see.
For this people's heart has grown dull, / and their ears are hard of hearing, / and they have shut their eyes; / so that they might not look with their eyes / and listen with their ears, / and understand with their heart and turn— / and I would heal them.

Matthew 25:18,25
Don't hide your talent in the ground.
v.18. But the one who had received the one talent went off and dug a hole in the ground and hid his master's money.
v.25. I was afraid, and I went and hid your talent in the ground.

Luke 6:44
You get back what you put out. You are what you pay attention to.
For each tree is known by its own fruit. Figs are not gathered from thorns, nor are grapes picked from a bramble bush.

Luke 15:11–32
Reevaluate your life (like the Prodigal Son).
v.16. He would gladly have filled himself with the pods that the pigs were eating; and no one gave him anything.
v.17. But when he came to himself he said, "How many of my father's hired hands have bread enough and to spare, but here I am dying of hunger!"
v.18. I will get up and go to my father, and I will say to him, "Father, I have sinned against heaven and before you."
v.21. Then the son said to him, "Father, I have sinned against heaven and before you; I am no longer worthy to be called your son."
v.22. "For this son of mine was dead and is alive again; he was lost and is found!" And they began to celebrate.

John 6:66
Do not give up. Don't turn back after you have started walking the spiritual journey.
Because of this many of his disciples turned back and no longer went about with him.

John 9:40–41
You brag about how well you see, but you are really fooled and blind.
v.40. Some of the Pharisees near him heard this and said to him, "Surely we are not blind, are we?"
v.41. Jesus said to them, "If you were blind, you would not have sin. But now that you say, 'We see,' your sin remains."

Acts 7:51
You even oppose the Holy Spirit in your heart.
You stiff-necked people, uncircumcised in heart and ears, you are forever opposing the Holy Spirit, just as your ancestors used to do.

Acts 28:27
You really didn't want to see, so you closed your eyes and your ears.
For this people's heart has grown dull, / and their ears are hard of hearing, / and they have shut their eyes; / so that they might not look with their eyes, / and listen with their ears, / and understand with their heart and turn— / and I would heal them.

Romans 2:5
Nothing seems to get past some people's stubbornness. You are not opening up to changing.
But by your hard and impenitent heart you are storing up wrath for yourself on the day of wrath, when God's righteous judgment will be revealed.

Romans 7:18–20
Ask for help, if you feel powerless, trapped, stuck.
v.18. For I know that nothing good dwells within me, that is, in my flesh. I can will what is right, but I cannot do it.
v.19. For I do not do the good I want, but the evil I do not want is what I do.
v.20. Now if I do what I do not want, it is no longer I that do it, but sin that dwells within me.

1 Corinthians 10:13
He can show you how to escape darkness' power and temptation.
No testing has overtaken you that is not common to everyone. God is faithful, and he will not let you be tested beyond your strength, but with the testing he will also provide the way out so that you may be able to endure it.

Ephesians 4:22–24
You are called to a spiritual revolution.
v.22. You were taught to put away your former way of life, your old self, corrupt and deluded by its lusts.
v.23. And to be renewed in the spirit of your minds.
v.24. And to clothe yourselves with the new self.

Ephesians 5:12
You appear to be one way, but you very different in your private life.
For it is shameful even to mention what such people do secretly.

Hebrews 11:34
Your real strength will be won when you know your weakness.
Quenched raging fire, escaped the edge of the sword, won strength out of weakness, became mighty in war, put foreign armies to flight.

2 Peter 1:8
You have to be careful to not let your patterns grow unchecked inside you.
For if these things are yours and are increasing among you, they keep you from being ineffective and unfruitful in the knowledge of our Lord Jesus Christ.

Revelation 3:17
You do not know that you are blind.
For you say, "I am rich, I have prospered, and I need nothing." You do not realize that you are wretched, pitiable, poor, blind, and naked.

Step Two: Belief

Exodus 15:26
I, the Lord, am your healer.
He said, "If you will listen carefully to the voice of the LORD your God, and do what is right in his sight, and give heed to his commandments and keep all his statutes, I will not bring upon you any of the diseases that I brought upon the Egyptians; for I am the LORD who heals you."

2 Samuel 22:31
God's way is true, a refuge.
This God—his way is perfect; / the promise of the LORD proves true; / he is a shield for all who take refuge in him.

1 Chronicles 5:20
If you believe, your prayers will be answered.
For they cried to God in the battle, and he granted their entreaty because they trusted in him.

Psalm 10:14
God is the helper of you when you need him most.
But you do see! Indeed you note trouble and grief, / that you may take it into your hands; / the helpless commit themselves to you; / you have been the helper of the orphan.

Psalm 18:30
God will help you. It is his way.
This God—his way is perfect; / the promise of the LORD proves true; / he is a shield for all who take refuge in him.

Psalm 32:10
If you can trust, you will find yourself experiencing love all around you.
Many are the torments of the wicked, / but steadfast love surrounds those who trust in the LORD.

Psalm 146:8
God will open your eyes.
The LORD opens the eyes of the blind. / The LORD lifts up those who are bowed down; / the LORD loves the righteous.

Isaiah 42:18
God will open your eyes.
Listen, you that are deaf; / and you that are blind, look up and see!

Isaiah 55:8–9
God's ways are not your ways.
v.8. For my thoughts are not your thoughts, / nor are your ways my ways, says the LORD.
v.9. For as the heavens are higher than the earth, / so are my ways higher than your ways / and my thoughts than your thoughts.

Jeremiah 29:12–13
God has told us to look for him, and we will find him.
v.12. Then when you call upon me and come and pray to me, I will hear you.
v.13. When you search for me, you will find me; if you seek me with all your heart.

Hosea 11:4
God's love is very tender and nurturing.
I led them with cords of human kindness, / with bands of love. / I was to them like those / who lift infants to their cheeks. / I bent down to them and fed them.

Zechariah 8:7
God is open to rescuing every one of you.
Thus says the LORD of hosts: I will save my people from the east country and from the west country.

Matthew 8:17
God will help you completely as you need, if you will trust.
This was to fulfill what had been spoken through the prophet Isaiah, "He took our infirmities and bore our diseases."

Matthew 9:20–22
Your faith has made you well.
v.20. Then suddenly a woman who had been suffering from hemorrhages for twelve years came up behind him and touched the fringe of his cloak.
v.21. For she said to herself, "If I only touch his cloak, I will be made well."
v.22. Jesus turned, and seeing her he said, "Take heart, daughter; your faith has made you well." And instantly the woman was made well.

Matthew 11:5
Even you blind can be helped to see.
The blind receive their sight, the lame walk, the lepers are cleansed, the deaf hear, the dead are raised, and the poor have good news brought to them.

Matthew 12:22
Real miracles can happen.
Then they brought to him a demoniac who was blind and mute; and he cured him, so that the one who had been mute could speak and see.

Matthew 14:25–32
Begin with faith, then go on.
v.25. And early in the morning he came walking toward them on the sea.
v.27. But immediately Jesus spoke to them and said, "Take heart, it is I; do not be afraid."
v.31. Jesus immediately reached out his hand and caught him, saying to him, "You of little faith, why did you doubt?"
v.32. When they got into the boat, the wind ceased.

Matthew 15:31
Even you blind can be helped if you are open to receive it.
So that the crowd was amazed when they saw the mute speaking, the maimed whole, the lame walking, and the blind seeing. And they praised the God of Israel.

Mark 8:22-26
Begin with faith, then go on. God will help you to see clearly.
v.22. They came to Bethsaida. Some people brought a blind man to him and begged him to touch him.
v.25. Then Jesus laid his hands on his eyes again; and he looked intently and his sight was restored, and he saw everything clearly.

Mark 9:24–25
Try to believe. God can heal you from any evil.
v.24. Immediately the father of the child cried out, "I believe; help my unbelief!"
v.25. Jesus…rebuked the unclean spirit, saying to it, "You spirit that keeps this boy from speaking and hearing, I command you, come out of him, and never enter him again!"

Luke 11:9
Seek God and you will find him.
So I say to you, Ask, and it will be given you; search, and you will find; knock, and the door will be opened for you.

John 9:40-41
God can heal your blindness.
v.40. Some of the Pharisees near him heard this and said to him, "Surely we are not blind, are we?"
v.41. Jesus said to them, "If you were blind, you would not have sin. But now that you say, 'We see,' your sin remains."

Romans 8:11
God's Spirit will give life to your body.
If the Spirit of him who raised Jesus from the dead dwells in you, he who raised Christ from the dead will give life to your mortal bodies also through his Spirit that dwells in you.

Romans 9:33
If you believe, you will not know disappointment.
As it is written, "See, I am laying in Zion a stone / that will make people stumble, a rock that will make them fall, / and whoever believes in him / will not be put to shame."

Romans 10:11
If you believe, you will not be disappointed.
The scripture says, "No one who believes in him will be put to shame."

1 Corinthians 15:43–44
You begin with a body and weakness. You can grow and evolve with great personal power.
v.43. It is sown in dishonor, it is raised in glory. It is sown in weakness, it is raised in power.
v.44. It is sown a physical body, it is raised a spiritual body. If there is a physical body, there is also a spiritual body.

Colossians 1:26
You can come to know God too.
The mystery that has been hidden throughout the ages and generations has now been revealed to his saints.

2 Timothy 2:13
He will carry you, help you, even if you are too weak.
If we are faithless, he remains faithful— / for he cannot deny himself.

2 Peter 2:9
The Lord knows how to rescue you from your trials, if you will trust him.
Then the Lord knows how to rescue the godly from trial, and to keep the unrighteous under punishment until the day of judgment.

Step Three: Decision, Commitment

Psalm 37:5
Commit yourself, your life to the Lord. He will help you.
Commit your way to the LORD; / trust in him, and he will act.

Psalm 50:15
God wants to support us, if we will let him.
Call on me in the day of trouble; / I will deliver you, and you shall glorify me.

Psalm 55:16
Call to God and he will save you.
But I call upon God, / and the LORD will save me.

Psalm 56:4,11
Put your trust in God, and nothing can harm you.
v.4. In God, whose word I praise, / in God I trust; I am not afraid; / what can flesh do to me?
v.11. In God I trust; I am not afraid. / What can a mere mortal do to me?

Isaiah 12:2
Trust God and you do not have to be afraid.
Surely God is my salvation; / I will trust, and will not be afraid, / for the LORD GOD is my strength and my might; / he has become my salvation.

Isaiah 30:21
If you listen, you will hear a gentle invitation to walk with him, his way.
And when you turn to the right or when you turn to the left, your ears shall hear a word behind you, saying, "This is the way; walk in it."

Isaiah 48:17
God wants to lead you, to teach you.
Thus says the LORD, / your Redeemer, the Holy One of Israel: / I am the LORD your God, / who teaches you for your own good, / who leads you in the way you should go.

Ezekiel 16:8
God wants to protect you, to love you.
I passed by you again and looked on you; you were at the age for love. I spread the edge of my cloak over you, and covered your nakedness: I pledged myself to you and entered into a covenant with you, says the Lord GOD, and you became mine.

Matthew 6:33-34
Trust God, one day at a time.
v.33. But strive first for the kingdom of God and his righteousness, and all these things will be given to you as well.
v.34. So do not worry about tomorrow, for tomorrow will bring worries of its own. Today's trouble is enough for today.

Matthew 11:30
Walking with God isn't so hard.
For my yoke is easy, and my burden is light.

John 14:6
Jesus wants us to walk his way, with him.
Jesus said to him, "I am the way, and the truth, and the life. No one comes to the Father except through me."

Acts 27:25
I will trust in God.
So keep up your courage, men, for I have faith in God that it will be exactly as I have been told.

2 Corinthians 5:7
If you see clearly, you don't need faith.
For we walk by faith, not by sight.

Ephesians 4:22
Put away your former way of life.
You were taught to put away your former way of life, your old self,
corrupt and deluded by its lusts.

James 4:7
Submit yourselves to God.
Submit yourselves therefore to God. Resist the devil, and he will flee from you.

Step Four: Examination, Inventory

1 Chronicles 28:9
God searches minds and hearts.
And you, my son Solomon, know the God of your father, and serve him with single mind and willing heart; for the LORD searches every mind, and understands every plan and thought. If you seek him, he will be found by you; but if you forsake him, he will abandon you forever.

Job 22:15
Give up your old path, your old way.
Will you keep to the old way / that the wicked have trod?

Proverbs 15:19
Give up your old path; God's is easier.
The way of the lazy is overgrown with thorns, / but the path of the upright is a level highway.

Proverbs 16:18
Be careful. Pride goes before disaster.
Pride goes before destruction, / and a haughty spirit before a fall.

Proverbs 23:19–21
Gluttony and drunkenness can reflect deep problems in your inner heart.
v.19. Hear, my child, and be wise, / and direct your mind in the way.
v.20. Do not be among winebibbers, / or among gluttonous eaters of meat.
v.21. For the drunkard and the glutton will come to poverty, / and drowsiness will clothe them with rags.

Jeremiah 17:10
I the Lord search your heart.
I the LORD test the mind / and search the heart, / to give to all according to their ways, / according to the fruit of their doings.

Jeremiah 18:15
Give up your own path. The bypath is not God's direction.
They have stumbled in their ways, / …and have gone into bypaths, / not the highway.

Matthew 5:21
Anger makes for judgment.
You have heard that it was said to those of ancient times, "You shall not murder"; and "whoever murders shall be liable to judgment."

Matthew 20:33
Ask God to open your eyes to be honest.
They said to him, "Lord, let our eyes be opened."

Mark 10:51
Ask God to help you to see.
Then Jesus said to him, "What do you want me to do for you?" The blind man said to him, "My teacher, let me see again."

Luke 6:24–26
Success and money won't meet your needs.
v.24. But woe to you who are rich, / for you have received your consolation.
v.25. Woe to you who are full now, / for you will be hungry. / Woe to you who are laughing now, / for you will mourn and weep.
v.26. Woe to you when all speak well of you, for that is what their ancestors did to the false prophets.

Luke 6:41–42
Reflect on your life, not your neighbor's life.
v.41. Why do you see the speck in your neighbor's eye, but do not notice the log in your own eye?
v.42. Or how can you say to your neighbor, "Friend, let me take out the speck in your eye," when you yourself do not see the log in your own eye? You hypocrite, first take the log out of your own eye, and then you will see clearly to take the speck out of your neighbor's eye.

Luke 18:41
Ask God to help you see.
"What do you want me to do for you?" He said, "Lord, let me see again."

John 15:2
God will help you to let go of those traits which are not bearing good fruit.
He removes every branch in me that bears no fruit. Every branch that bears fruit he prunes to make it bear more fruit.

Romans 12:6–8
You do have gifts. It is important to look at yourself honestly, to open up to your gifts being increased.
v.6. We have gifts that differ according to the grace given to us: prophecy, in proportion to our faith.
v.7. Ministry, in ministering; the teacher, in teaching.
v.8. The exhorter, in exhortation; the giver, in generosity; the leader, in diligence; the compassionate, in cheerfulness.

1 Corinthians 4:5
Your task is to look at your own heart, not to judge anyone else.
Therefore do not pronounce judgment before the time, before the Lord comes, who will bring to light the things now hidden in darkness and will disclose the purposes of the heart. Then each one will receive commendation from God.

1 Corinthians 6:12–13
Do not become enslaved by things, by gluttony, and temperance.
v.12. "All things are lawful for me," but not all things are beneficial. "All things are lawful for me," but I will not be dominated by anything.
v.13. Food is meant for the stomach and the stomach for food, and God will

destroy both one and the other. The body is meant not for fornication but for the Lord, and the Lord for the body.

1 Corinthians 14:25
Let God show you the darkness in your heart.
After the secrets of the unbeliever's heart are disclosed, that person will bow down before God and worship him.

2 Corinthians 7:1
Cleanse yourself from every thing that defiles.
Since we have these promises, beloved, let us cleanse ourselves from every defilement of body and of spirit, making holiness perfect in the fear of God.

Philippians 2:3
Humble yourself, look at your motives.
Do nothing from selfish ambition or conceit, but in humility regard others as better than yourselves.

Philippians 3:19
Look honestly at your drives, your motives.
Their end is destruction; their god is the belly; and their glory is in their shame; their minds are set on earthly things.

2 Timothy 2:21
Cleanse yourself and let God use you for his good work.
All who cleanse themselves of the things I have mentioned will become special utensils, dedicated and useful to the owner of the house, ready for every good work.

Hebrews 12:13
Give up your old path. It is crippling you and making you sick.
Make straight paths for your feet, so that what is lame may not be put out of joint, but rather be healed.

1 John 3:17
Be just with others.
How does God's love abide in anyone who has the world's goods and sees a brother or sister in need and yet refuses help?

Step Five: Admit Your Defects

Leviticus 5:5,16
It is important to tell someone your darkness.
v.5. When you realize your guilt in any of these, you shall confess the sin that you have committed.
vs.5,16. Confess the sin that you have committed....you shall make restitution for the holy thing in which you were remiss, and shall add one-fifth to it, and give it to the priest.

Jeremiah 3:13
Only acknowledge your wrong.
Only acknowledge your guilt, / that you have rebelled against the LORD your God, / and scattered your favors among strangers under every green tree, / and have not obeyed my voice, says the LORD.

Acts 19:18
To remain as a believer it is necessary to disclose your wrongs, and to let go of them.
Also many of those who became believers confessed and disclosed their practices.

1 Corinthians 14:25
Admitting your wrongs is the beginning of the relationship with God.
After the secrets of the unbeliever's heart are disclosed, that person will bow down before God and worship him, declaring, "God is really among you."

James 5:16
Confess your sins to each other.
Therefore confess your sins to one another, and pray for one another, so that you may be healed.

1 John 1:9
If you confess your sins, he will forgive you.
If we confess our sins, he who is faithful and just will forgive us our sins and cleanse us from all unrighteousness.

Step Six: Become Ready to Ask

Exodus 10:3
Don't be "stiff-necked" like Pharaoh.
How long will you refuse to humble yourself before me?

2 Samuel 13:13
You have to be ready to let go of your shame.
As for me, where could I carry my shame?

Acts 3:19–20
Change your mind and your attitude, so you can receive the new spiritual experience of God.
v.19. Repent therefore, and turn to God so that your sins may be wiped out.
v.20. So that times of refreshing may come from the presence of the Lord, and that he may send the Messiah appointed for you.

1 Peter 2:24
He carried our load so that we can be finished with sin.
He himself bore our sins in his body on the cross, so that, free from sins, we might live for righteousness; by his wounds you have been healed.

Step Seven: Ask for Release

2 Kings 20:5
You prayed, I have heard you.
Thus says the LORD, the God of your ancestor David: I have heard your prayer, I have seen your tears; indeed, I will heal you; on the third day you shall go up to the house of the LORD.

Psalm 51:2,7
Ask God to wash you clean from your defects.
v.2. Wash me thoroughly from my iniquity, / and cleanse me from my sin.
v.7. Purge me with hyssop, and I shall be clean; / wash me, and I shall be whiter than snow.

Isaiah 4:4
God can remove your stains.
Once the Lord has washed away the filth of the daughters of Zion and cleansed the bloodstains of Jerusalem from its midst by a spirit of judgment and by a spirit of burning.

Ezekiel 36:25
God will wash you completely clean.
I will sprinkle clean water upon you, and you shall be clean from all your uncleannesses, and from all your idols I will cleanse you.

Matthew 8:2
Ask God to make you clean.
And there was a leper who came to him and knelt before him, saying, "Lord, if you choose, you can make me clean."

Matthew 18:1–4
Turn to God. Humble yourself.
v.4. Whoever becomes humble like this child is the greatest in the kingdom of heaven.

Mark 1:40
Ask God to make you clean.
A leper came to him begging him, and kneeling he said to him, "If you choose, you can make me clean."

Mark 11:24
What you ask in prayer, believe you will receive.
So I tell you, whatever you ask for in prayer, believe that you have received it, and it will be yours.

Luke 5:12
Ask God to make you clean.
Once, when he was in one of the cities, there was a man covered with leprosy. When he saw Jesus, he bowed with his face to the ground and begged him, "Lord, if you choose, you can make me clean."

Acts 3:19–20
Change your mind and attitude.
Repent therefore, and turn to God so that your sins may be wiped out.

Ephesians 4:22
Put away your old self, your corrupt, deluded self.
You were taught to put away your former way of life, your old self, corrupt and deluded by its lusts.

1 Peter 2:24
He carried your load, so that you can be finished with sin.
He himself bore our sins in his body on the cross, so that, free from sins, we might live for righteousness; by his wounds you have been healed.

Step Eight: Make Amends List

Leviticus 5:5,7
It is important to tell someone your darkness.
v.5. When you realize your guilt in any of these, you shall confess the sin that you have committed.
v.7. But if you cannot afford a sheep, you shall bring to the LORD, as your penalty for the sin that you have committed, two turtledoves or two pigeons, one for a sin offering and the other for a burnt offering.

Matthew 5:23–24
Go, and apologize.
v.23. So when you are offering your gift at the altar, if you remember that your brother or sister has something against you.
v.24. Leave your gift there before the altar and go; first be reconciled to your brother and sister, and then come and offer your gift.

Matthew 6:14–15
Forgive others, and you will be forgiven.
v.14. For if you forgive others their trespasses, your heavenly Father will also forgive you.
v.15. But if you do not forgive others, neither will your Father forgive your trespasses.

Matthew 18:21–25
You must prepare your accounting of what you owe to others.
v.23. For this reason the kingdom of heaven may be compared to a king who wished to settle accounts with his slaves.
v.24. When he began the reckoning, one who owed him ten thousand talents was brought to him.

Luke 17:4
Prepare to be forgiven, but develop a forgiving attitude as well.
And if the same person sins against you seven times a day, and turns back to you seven times and says, "I repent," you must forgive.

Step Nine: List of Amends

Exodus 21 and 22
You must make restitution for the wrongs you have done to others.

Leviticus 5:5,16
It is important to tell someone your darkness.
v.5. When you realize your guilt in any of these, you shall confess the sin that you have committed.
v.5,16. Confess the sin that you have committed....you shall make restitution for the holy thing in which you were remiss, and shall add one-fifth to it and give it to the priest.

Proverbs 6:31
Thief must repay.
Yet if they are caught, they will pay sevenfold; / they will forfeit all the goods of their house.

Matthew 5:23–24
Go, and apologize.
v.23. So when you are offering your gift at the altar, if you remember that your brother or sister has something against you.
v.24. Leave your gift there before the altar and go; first be reconciled to your brother or sister, and then come and offer your gift.

Luke 17:4
Your responsibility is to make your amends, and receive those of others.
And if the same person sins against you seven times a day, and turns back to you seven times and says, "I repent," you must forgive.

Romans 13:7–8
Pay all your debts.
v.7. Pay to all what is due them—taxes to whom taxes are due, revenue to whom revenue is due, respect to whom respect is due, honor to whom honor is due.
v.8. Owe no one anything, except to love one another; for the one who loves another has fulfilled the law.

Step Ten: Maintain Growth

Exodus 33:13
Ask for help to keep on learning his way.
Now if I have found favor in your sight, show me your ways, so that I may know you and find favor in your sight. Consider too that this nation is your people.

Psalm 86:11
Ask for help to keep on learning how to walk with an undivided heart.
Teach me your way, O LORD, / that I may walk in your truth; / give me an undivided heart to revere your name.

Isaiah 2:3
Be eager to keep on learning your new way.
Many peoples shall come and say, / "Come, let us go up to the mountain of the LORD, / to the house of the God of Jacob; / that he may teach us his ways / and that we may walk in his paths." / For out of Zion shall go forth instruction, / and the word of the LORD from Jerusalem.

Matthew 25:3
You must continue to be prepared and vigilant as you walk his new walk.
The foolish virgins took no oil with them.

1 Corinthians 9:16–17
Live your new spiritual awareness. Remember a fully trained pupil will be like his teacher.
v.16. If I proclaim the gospel, this gives me no ground for boasting, for an obligation is laid on me, and woe to me if I do not proclaim the gospel!
v.17. For if I do this of my own will, I have a reward; but if not of my own will, I am entrusted with a commission.

Colossians 3:11
Act constantly more like Christ.
In that renewal there is no longer Greek and Jew, circumcised and uncircumcised, barbarian, Scythian, slave and free; but Christ is all and in all!

1 Timothy 4:14
Do not neglect the spiritual gift within you.
Do not neglect the gift that is in you, which was given to you through prophecy with the laying on of hands by the council of elders.

2 Timothy 1:6
Rekindle the gift of God inside you.
For this reason I remind you to rekindle the gift of God that is within you through the laying on of my hands.

Hebrews 3:12
Be careful to nurture your own life.
Take care, brothers and sisters, that none of you may have an evil, unbelieving heart that turns away from the living God.

James 1:27
True religion means to practice your new spiritual awareness in your daily life.
Religion that is pure and undefiled before God, the Father, is this: to care for orphans and widows in their distress, and to keep oneself unstained by the world.

1 Peter 1:14
It is easy to do, but do not return to your former ignorant passions.
Like obedient children, do not be conformed to the desires that you formerly had in ignorance.

Step Eleven: Conscious Contact (Prayer)

2 Kings 19:20
You prayed, I have heard you.
Thus says the LORD, the God of Israel: I have heard your prayer to me about King Sennacherib of Assyria.

2 Kings 20:5
God promises to hear us, and to answer our prayer.
Thus says the LORD, the God of your ancestor David: "I have heard your prayer, I have seen your tears; indeed, I will heal you; on the third day you shall go up to the house of the LORD."

Psalm 22:26
When you who seek God you will find yourself also praising him.
The poor shall eat and be satisfied; / those who seek him shall praise the LORD. / May your hearts live forever!

Psalm 50:15
God tells us to call on him when we have trouble.
Call on me in the day of trouble; / I will deliver you, and you shall glorify me.

Jeremiah 29:12–13
Pray to me, I will listen.
v.12. Then when you call upon me and come and pray to me, I will hear you.
v.13. When you search for me, you will find me; if you seek me with all your heart.

Jeremiah 33:3
God is waiting for you. He has wonderful things to give you.
Call to me and I will answer you, and will tell you great and hidden things that you have not known.

Lamentations 3:41
When you pray, lift up your heart and hands.
Let us lift up our hearts as well as our hands / to God in heaven.

Daniel 6:18
Sometimes when you pray, also fast and practice discipline which is hard for you.
Then the king went to his palace and spent the night fasting; no food was brought to him, and sleep fled from him.

Matthew 5:44
Pray for anyone who is making your life difficult for you.
But I say to you, Love your enemies and pray for those who persecute you.

Matthew 6:5–7
Jesus gives an instruction on how to pray. Try the privacy of your own room of solitude.
v.5. And whenever you pray, do not be like the hypocrites; for they love to stand and pray in the synagogues and at the street corners, so that they may be seen by others. Truly I tell you, they have received their reward.
v.6. But whenever you pray, go into your room and shut the door and pray to your Father who is in secret; and your Father who sees in secret will reward you.
v.7. When you are praying, do not heap up empty phrases as the Gentiles do; for they think that they will be heard because of their many words.

Matthew 6:9–14
Jesus gives another way to pray.
v.9. Pray then in this way: / Our Father in heaven, / hallowed be your name.
v.10. Your kingdom come. / Your will be done, / on earth as it is in heaven.
v.11. Give us this day our daily bread.
v.12. And forgive us our debts, / as we also have forgiven our debtors.
v.13. And do not bring us to the time of trial, / but rescue us from the evil one.
v.14. For if you forgive others their trespasses, your heavenly Father will also forgive you.

Matthew 6:18
God also invites us to practice doing "hard things," developing personal discipline.
So that your fasting may be seen not by others but by your Father who is in secret; and your Father who sees in secret will reward you.

Matthew 21:22
What you ask in prayer, believe, and you will receive.
Whatever you ask for in prayer with faith, you will receive.

Mark 11:24
What you ask in prayer, believe, you will receive.
So I tell you, whatever you ask for in prayer, believe that you have received it, and it will be yours.

Luke 5:16
When you pray, withdraw in solitude.
But he would withdraw to deserted places and pray.

Luke 6:28
Pray for those who harm you.
Bless those who curse you, pray for those who abuse you.

Luke 11:1–4
Jesus gives a teaching on how to pray.
v.1. He was praying in a certain place, and after he had finished, one of his disciples said to him, "Lord, teach us to pray, as John taught his disciples."
v.2. He said to them, "When you pray, say: / Father, hallowed be your name. / Your kingdom come."
v.3. "Give us each day our daily bread."
v.4. "And forgive us our sins, / for we ourselves forgive everyone indebted to us. / And do not bring us to the time of trial."

Luke 11:9
Seek God and you will find him.
So I say to you, Ask, and it will be given you; search, and you will find; knock, and the door will be opened for you.

John 4:23,24
Let your life and actions show others what you believe and pray.
v.23. But the hour is coming, and is now here, when the true worshipers will worship the Father in spirit and truth, for the Father seeks such as these to worship him.
v.24. God is spirit, and those who worship him must worship in spirit and truth.

Romans 12:12
Keep at it. Don't become discouraged. Persevere with your prayers.
Rejoice in hope, be patient in suffering, persevere in prayer.

1 Corinthians 14:14
Praying in "tongues" is one way to pray. The mind has no control of your worship.
For if I pray in a tongue, my spirit prays but my mind is unproductive.

1 Corinthians 14:15
You can also sing praise with your spirit and with your mind.
What should I do then? I will pray with the spirit, but I will pray with the mind also; I will sing praise with the spirit, but I will sing praise with the mind also.

1 Timothy 2:8
God says to live in such a way that your life is a prayer wherever you are. Live with your heart free from sin and arguing.
I desire, then, that in every place the men should pray, lifting up holy hands without anger or argument.

2 Timothy 1:6
Rekindle the gift of God inside you.
For this reason I remind you to rekindle the gift of God that is within you.

Step Twelve: Share

Proverbs 25:25
Share humbly with others your new experience of God. Good news is like cold water to the thirsty.
Like cold water to a thirsty soul, / so is good news from a far country.

Ecclesiastes 4:10
Practice these principles in all your affairs. If one falls, help him.
For if they fall, one will lift up the other.

Jeremiah 17:8
If this spiritual awareness is really yours, you will yield its fruit continually.
They shall be like a tree planted by water, / sending out its roots by the stream. / It shall not fear when heat comes, / and its leaves shall stay green; / in the year of drought it is not anxious, / and it does not cease to bear fruit.

Matthew 5:14–16
Bring forth fruit that reflects your new conversion.
v.14. You are the light of the world. A city built on a hill cannot be hid.
v.15. No one after lighting a lamp puts it under the bushel basket, but on the lampstand, and it gives light to all in the house.
v.16. In the same way, let your light shine before others, so that they may see your good works and give glory to your Father in heaven.

Matthew 5:19
Your own spiritual experience is not enough. You must also be willing to "walk the walk," and share with others too.
Therefore, whoever breaks one of the least of these commandments, and teaches others to do the same, will be called least in the kingdom of heaven; but whoever does them and teaches them will be called great in the kingdom of heaven.

Matthew 6:4,6,18
When you do good works, don't flaunt them or brag about it.
v.4. So that your alms may be done in secret; and your Father who sees in secret will reward you.

Matthew 7:16–20
You don't have to brag or impose your good news on others. They will see it themselves by how you live.
v.16. You will know them by their fruits. Are grapes gathered from thorns, or figs from thistles?
v.17. In the same way, every good tree bears good fruit, but the bad tree bears bad fruit.
v.18. A good tree cannot bear bad fruit, nor can a bad tree bear good fruit.
v.19. Every tree that does not bear good fruit is cut down and thrown into the fire.
v.20. Thus you will know them by their fruits.

Luke 3:8
Let your life reflect your new way, your new inheritance, your new repentance.
Bear fruits worthy of repentance. Do not begin to say to yourselves, "We have Abraham as our ancestor"; for I tell you, God is able from these stones to raise up children to Abraham.

John 15:16
You are now expected to serve others, help them, be good news for the earth.
You did not choose me but I chose you. And I appointed you to go and bear fruit, fruit that will last, so that the Father will give you whatever you ask him in my name.

Acts 2:42
Keep contact with others for support in your new way of life.
They devoted themselves to the apostles' teaching and fellowship, to the breaking of bread and the prayers.

Romans 10:14
It is essential that you pass on this message to others.
But how are they to call on one in whom they have not believed? And how are they to believe in one of whom they have never heard? And how are they to hear without someone to proclaim him?

Romans 12:9–10
Your new way of seeing is to be shown to others with love and respect for them.
v.9. Let love be genuine; hate what is evil, hold fast to what is good.
v.10. Love one another with mutual affection; outdo one another in showing honor.

Romans 16:2
Welcome those who do not yet have what you have. Receive them, and encourage them gently with compassion, not judgment.
So that you may welcome her in the Lord as is fitting for the saints, and help her in whatever she may require from you, for she has been a benefactor of many and of myself as well.

1 Corinthians 9:16–17
Live your new spiritual awareness.
v.16. If I proclaim the gospel, this gives me no ground for boasting, for an obligation is laid on me, and woe to me if I do not proclaim the Gospel!
v.17. For if I do this of my own will, I have a reward; but not of my own will, I am entrusted with a commission.

1 Corinthians 13:4–7
If you really have the spiritual awakening, it will show in your living the "program."
v.4. Love is patient, love is kind; love is not envious or boastful or arrogant.
v.5. Or rude. It does not insist on its own way; it is not irritable or resentful.
v.6. It does not rejoice in wrongdoing, but rejoices in the truth.
v.7. It bears all things, believes all things, hopes all things, endures all things.

Galatians 2:9
As you grow, extend fellowship and support to those who are beginning the walk, as well as those who are continuing.
And when James and Cephas and John, who were acknowledged pillars, recognized the grace that had been given to me, they gave to Barnabas and me the right hand of fellowship.

Philippians 1:27
Conduct yourselves in a manner that shows your spiritual program at work.
Only, live your life in a manner worthy of the gospel of Christ, so that, whether I come and see you or am absent and hear about you, I will know that you are standing firm in one spirit, striving side by side with one mind for the faith of the gospel.

Colossians 1:10
Bear fruit by doing good work.
So that you may lead lives worthy of the Lord, fully pleasing to him, as you bear fruit in every good work and as you grow in the knowledge of God.

Colossians 2:6
You have received the spiritual way, the "Steps"; practice them.
As you therefore have received Christ Jesus the Lord, continue to live your lives in him.

2 Timothy 1:6,7-8
Never be afraid to tell others about your experience.
v.6. For this reason I remind you to rekindle the gift of God that is within you.
v.7. For God did not give us a spirit of cowardice, but rather a spirit of power and of love and of self-discipline.
v.8. Do not be ashamed, then, of the testimony about our Lord or of me his prisoner, but join with me in suffering for the gospel, relying on the power of God.

Titus 2:7
Give example by your actions.
Show yourself in all respects a model of good works, and in your teaching show integrity, gravity.

Hebrews 13:16
Be careful to look always for ways to serve others, and to practice your program in all your affairs.
Do not neglect to do good and to share what you have, for such sacrifices are pleasing to God.

James 1:26
You are kidding yourself if you think you are living a spiritual program if your tongue is cruel.
If any think they are religious, and do not bridle their tongues but deceive their hearts, their religion is worthless.

James 1:27
You are kidding yourself if you are not serving others, and practicing your spiritual program in all your affairs, in your daily life.
Religion that is pure and undefiled before God, the Father, is this: to care for orphans and widows in their distress, and to keep oneself unstained by the world.

1 Peter 4:8–10
Live your life, using your gifts to serve each other.
v.8. Above all, maintain constant love for one another, for love covers a multitude of sins.
v.9. Be hospitable to one another without complaining.
v.10. Like good stewards of the manifold grace of God, serve one another with whatever gift each of you has received.

1 John 1:3–7
One of the proofs of a solid spiritual life is a lived relationship, supporting and encouraging one another.
v.3. We declare to you what we have seen and heard so that you also may have fellowship with us; and truly our fellowship is with the Father and with his Son Jesus Christ.
v.6. If we say that we have fellowship with him while we are walking in darkness, we lie and do not do what is true.
v.7. But if we walk in the light as he himself is in the light, we have fellowship with one another, and the blood of Jesus his Son cleanses us from all sin.

1 John 5:16
Pray for each other as you err.
If you see your brother or sister committing what is not a mortal sin, you will ask, and God will give life to such a one—to those whose sin is not mortal. There is sin that is mortal; I do not say that you should pray about that.

Appendix 5

Scriptures and Enneagram Points

These references are offered for your prayer and reflection with the Enneagram.

Point One: Perfectionist, Need to Be Perfect

Passion: Anger; resentment

Psalm 37:8
An angry, resentful heart is no good.
Refrain from anger, and forsake wrath. / Do not fret—it leads only to evil.

Proverbs 29:8
You are invited to turn away from your anger.
Scoffers set a city aflame, / but the wise turn away wrath.

Ecclesiastes 7:9
You are a fool if you are living with anger always in your heart.
Do not be quick to anger, / for anger lodges in the bosom of fools.

Luke 15:28
Anger frequently does no good, and makes for confusion.
Then he became angry and refused to go in. His father came out and began to plead with him.

Romans 4:15
Resentments can develop when we are self-righteous in our judgments of the good.
For the law brings wrath; but where there is no law, neither is there violation.

1 Corinthians 13:5
If you think you have love, and you are full of resentment and irritable, think again.
It does not insist on its own way; it is not irritable or resentful.

Ephesians 4:31
Get rid of your anger.
Put away from you all bitterness and wrath and anger and wrangling and slander, together with all malice.

Colossians 3:8
Love is not irritable and hard to be around.
But now you must get rid of all such things—anger, wrath, malice, slander, and abusive language from your mouth.

James 1:20
Your anger does not show God to others.
For your anger does not produce God's righteousness.

Virtue: Serenity, cheerful tranquility

Isaiah 48:18
If you were living your spiritual awakening, your peace would flow like a river.
O that you had paid attention to my commandments! / Then your prosperity would have been like a river, / and your success like the waves of the sea.

Proverbs 4:18
Your spiritual path will guide others like the light of dawn, or a good road for them to use to find their way.
But the path of the righteous is like the light of dawn, / which shines brighter and brighter until full day.

Proverbs 15:19
The spiritual path of the upright is a smooth road.
The way of the lazy is overgrown with thorns, / but the path of the upright is a level highway.

Matthew 5:6
If you really hunger and thirst for that which is truly good, you will be satisfied.
Blessed are those who hunger and thirst for righteousness, for they will be filled.

Mark 9:50
God has called you to know peace.
Salt is good; but if salt has lost its saltiness, how can you season it? Have salt in yourselves, and be at peace with one another.

Romans 8:6
Set your mind on the Spirit and you will know a new life and peace.
To set the mind on the flesh is death, but to set the mind on the Spirit is life and peace.

Romans 12:18
Be at peace with everyone.
If it is possible, so far as it depends on you, live peaceably with all.

1 Corinthians 7:15
God has called you to peace, no matter how others around you choose or act.
But if the unbelieving partner separates, let it be so; in such a case the brother or sister is not bound. It is to peace that God has called you.

Colossians 3:15
Let the peace of Christ rule in your hearts.
And let the peace of Christ rule in your hearts, to which indeed you were called in the one body. And be thankful.

James 3:17
Real serenity is very precious. God's wisdom from above is flexible, peace-filled, merciful.
But the wisdom from above is first pure, then peaceable, gentle, willing to yield, full of mercy and good fruits, without a trace of partiality or hypocrisy.

1 Peter 3:11
Seek peace and pursue it.
Let them turn away from evil and do good; / let them seek peace and pursue it.

Point Two: The Giver

Passion: Pride, false love

Exodus 10:3
Accept to look honestly at how you are living, and your love for others.
Thus says the LORD, the God of the Hebrews, "How long will you refuse to humble yourself before me?"

Psalm 17:10
Don't brag. Love gently.
They close their hearts to pity; / with their mouths they speak arrogantly.

Psalm 17:10
Evildoers speak arrogantly.
They close their hearts to pity; / with their mouths they speak arrogantly.

Psalm 49:6
You trust in your own ability to do things, your own wealth, talents, skills. They are not enough, and they will fail you.
Those who trust in their wealth / and boast of the abundance of their riches?

Psalm 52:7
You trust in your own wealth, talents, skills, and these won't last.
See the one who would not take refuge in God, / but trusted in abundant riches, / and sought refuge in wealth!

Psalm 62:10
Don't trust the things you can acquire.
If riches increase, do not set your heart on them.

Proverbs 11:28
Don't trust in yourself or in what you can acquire. This won't last.
Those who trust in their riches will wither, / but the righteous will flourish like green leaves.

Proverbs 21:4
It indicates a sinful heart if your manner is haughty and your heart proud.
Haughty eyes and a proud heart / the lamp of the wicked—are sin.

Ezekiel 16:15
You trusted in your beauty.
But you trusted in your beauty, and played the whore because of your fame, and lavished your whorings on any passer-by.

Matthew 10:8
Don't have strings attached to your giving.
Cure the sick, raise the dead, cleanse the lepers, cast out demons. You received without payment; give without payment.

Mark 7:20–23
How you act shows your true heart, the real you.
v.20. It is what comes out of a person that defiles.
v.21. For it is from within, from the human heart, that evil intentions come: fornication, theft, murder.
v.22. Adultery, avarice, wickedness, deceit, licentiousness, envy, slander, pride, folly.
v.23. All these evil things come from within, and they defile a person.

Romans 11:18
Do not be arrogant toward each other.
Do not boast over the branches. If you do boast, remember that it is not you that support the root, but the root that supports you.

Romans 12:3
Do not think of yourself more highly than you ought.
For by the grace given to me I say to everyone among you not to think of yourself more highly than you ought to think, but to think with sober judgment, each according to the measure of faith that God has assigned.

1 Corinthians 8:1
Knowledge puffs up, but love builds up.
Now concerning food sacrificed to idols: we know that "all of us possess knowledge." Knowledge puffs up, but love builds up.

1 Corinthians 13:4
True love is kind and gentle.
Love is patient; love is kind; love is not envious or boastful or arrogant.

Philippians 2:3
Do nothing out of any vain conceit.
Do nothing from selfish ambition or conceit, but in humility regard others as better than yourselves.

1 Timothy 6:17
You trust in your own wealth, talents, skills, and these will fail you.
As for those who in the present age are rich, command them not to be haughty, or to set their hopes on the uncertainty of riches, but rather on God who richly provides us with everything for our enjoyment.

Virtue: Humility, freedom of will

Leviticus 19:18
Love your neighbor as you love yourself.
You shall not take vengeance or bear a grudge against any of your people, but you shall love your neighbor as yourself: I am the LORD.

Proverbs 11:2
With the humble is wisdom.
When pride comes, then comes disgrace; / but wisdom is with the humble.

Proverbs 12:9
Better that you be humble than honor yourself.
Better to be despised and have a servant, / than to be self-important and lack food.

Proverbs 15:33
Humility goes before honor.
The fear of the Lord is instruction in wisdom, / and humility goes before honor.

Proverbs 18:12
Humility goes before honor.
Before destruction one's heart is haughty, / but humility goes before honor.

Proverbs 29:23
It is the humble who will receive honor.
A person's pride will bring humiliation, / but one who is lowly in spirit will obtain honor.

Micah 6:8
Walk humbly with your God.
He has told you, O mortal, what is good; / and what does the Lord require of you / but to do justice, and to love kindness, / and to walk humbly with your God?

Matthew 19:19
Love your neighbor as you love yourself.
Honor your father and mother; also, You shall love your neighbor as yourself.

Matthew 22:39
Love your neighbor as you love yourself.
And a second is like it: "You shall love your neighbor as yourself."

Mark 12:31
Love your neighbor as you love yourself.
The second is this, "You shall love your neighbor as yourself." There is no other commandment greater than these.

Luke 1:52
Let God teach you.
He has brought down the powerful from their thrones, / and lifted up the lowly.

Luke 10:27
Love your neighbor as you love yourself.
He answered, "You shall love the Lord your God with all your heart, and with all your soul, and with all your strength, and with all your mind; and your neighbor as yourself."

Luke 14:10
At a feast, take the lowest place.
But when you are invited, go and sit down at the lowest place, so that when your host comes, he may say to you, "Friend, move up higher"; then you will be honored in the presence of all who sit at the table with you.

John 5:42
You do not have the love of God in your hearts.
But I know that you do not have the love of God in you.

John 8:36
If the Son makes you free, you shall be free indeed.
So if the Son makes you free, you will be free indeed.

Romans 12:9
Let your love be sincere.
Let love be genuine; hate what is evil, hold fast to what is good.

Romans 12:16
Do not be proud. Associate with those you might think of as lowly.
Live in harmony with one another; do not be haughty, but associate with the lowly; do not claim to be wiser than you are.

Romans 13:9
Love your neighbor as you love yourself.
The commandments, "You shall not commit adultery; You shall not murder; You shall not steal; You shall not covet"; and any other commandment, are summed up in this word, "Love your neighbor as yourself."

1 Corinthians 3:9
Be a co-worker with God.
For we are God's servants, working together; you are God's field, God's building.

1 Corinthians 8:1
Knowledge puffs up, but love builds up.
Now...we know that all of us possess knowledge. Knowledge puffs up, but love builds up.

1 Corinthians 16:14
Do everything in love.
Let all that you do be done in love.

2 Corinthians 3:17
Where the Spirit of the Lord is, there is freedom.
Now the Lord is the Spirit, and where the Spirit of the Lord is, there is freedom.

2 Corinthians 9:7
Give to others with a free heart.
Each of you must give as you have made up your mind, not reluctantly or under compulsion, for God loves a cheerful giver.

Galatians 5:14
Love your neighbor as you love yourself.
For the whole law is summed up in a single commandment, "You shall love your neighbor as yourself."

Philippians 2:3
In humility consider others better than yourself.
Do nothing from selfish ambition or conceit, but in humility regard others as better than yourselves.

1 Timothy 5:10
Your love is seen in your good works.
She must be well attested for her good works, as one who has brought up children, shown hospitality, washed the saints' feet, helped the afflicted, and devoted herself to doing good in every way.

Hebrews 7:7
The lesser is blessed by the greater.
It is beyond dispute that the inferior is blessed by the superior.

Hebrews 13:2
Let your love show welcome to everyone, for you may be entertaining angels.
Do not neglect to show hospitality to strangers, for by doing that some have entertained angels without knowing it.

James 1:27
True religion is to visit orphans and widows.
Religion that is pure and undefiled before God, the Father, is this: to care for orphans and widows in their distress, and to keep oneself unstained by the world.

1 Peter 5:2
Care for each other generously and freely.
To tend the flock of God that is in your charge, exercising the oversight, not under compulsion but willingly, as God would have you do it—not for sordid gain but eagerly.

1 Peter 5:5–6
Put on the clothes of humility.
v.5. In the same way, you who are younger must accept the authority of the elders. And all of you must clothe yourselves with humility in your dealings with one another, for "God opposes the proud, / but gives grace to the humble."
v.6. Humble yourselves therefore under the mighty hand of God, so that he may exalt you in due time.

1 John 3:14
You are a living dead person if you don't love each other.
We know that we have passed from death to life because we love one another. Whoever does not love abides in death.

1 John 3:18–23
Let us love in action and in truth.
v.18. Little children, let us love, not in word or speech, but in truth and action.

v.19. *And by this we will know that we are from the truth and will reassure our hearts before him.*

v.20. *Whenever our hearts condemn us; for God is greater than our hearts, and he knows everything.*

v.21. *Beloved, if our hearts do not condemn us, we have boldness before God.*

v.22. *And we receive from him whatever we ask, because we obey his commandments and do what pleases him.*

v.23. *And this is his commandment, that we should believe in the name of his Son Jesus Christ and love one another, just as he has commanded us.*

Point Three: The Performer

Passion: Self-deceit, vanity

Job 13:9
Don't be deceived. Know what is really in your heart.
Will it be well with you when he searches you out? / Or can you deceive him, as one person deceives another?

Psalm 32:2
Happy are you if your spirit has no deceit.
Happy are those to whom the LORD imputes no iniquity, / and in whose spirit there is no deceit.

Psalm 49:6
You trust in your own ability to do things, your own wealth, talents, skills. They are not enough, and they will fail you.
Those who trust in their wealth / and boast of the abundance of their riches?

Psalm 52:7
You trust in your own wealth, talents, skills, and these won't last.
See the one who would take refuge in God, / but trusted in abundant riches, / and sought refuge in wealth!

Psalm 62:10
If you have success, and your wealth increases, do not set your heart on it.
If riches increase, do not set your heart on them.

Psalm 146:3
You are foolish, and you will fail if you trust in riches, success, other people.
Do not put your trust in princes, / in mortals, in whom there is no help.

Proverbs 11:28
Riches will not make your life meaningful.
Those who trust in their riches will wither, / but the righteous will flourish like green leaves.

Proverbs 23:5
You can lose things and wealth.
When your eyes light upon it, it is gone; / for suddenly it takes wings to itself, / flying like an eagle toward heaven.

Proverbs 27:24
Riches do not last forever.
For riches do not last forever, / nor a crown for all generations.

Isaiah 42:17
Think carefully about what you hold as your god.
They shall be turned back and utterly put to shame— / those who trust in carved images, / who say to cast images, / "You are our gods."

Jeremiah 17:5
You are foolish if you put your focus on riches, success, or other people.
Thus says the LORD: / Cursed are those who trust in mere mortals / and make mere flesh their strength, / whose hearts turn away from the LORD.

Jeremiah 17:9
We can deceive ourselves easily.
The heart is devious above all else; / it is perverse— / who can understand it?

Jeremiah 48:7
Be careful if your security is based on riches, success, or others.
Surely, because you trusted in your strongholds and your treasures, / you also shall be taken.

Matthew 6:21
What you focus on shows what you value.
For where your treasure is, there your heart will be also.

Matthew 13:22
Riches and pleasures can deceive you and choke the word in your heart.
As for what was sown among thorns, this is the one who hears the word, but the cares of the world and the lure of wealth choke the word, and it yields nothing.

Mark 4:19
Worry about security, and the drive for success can choke the word in your heart.
But the cares of the world, and the lure of wealth, and the desire for other things come in and choke the word, and it yields nothing.

Mark 7:20–23
How you act shows your true heart, the real you.
v.20. It is what comes out of a person that defiles.
v.21. For it is from within, from the human heart, that evil intentions come: fornication, theft, murder.
v.22. Adultery, avarice, wickedness, deceit, licentiousness, envy, slander, pride, folly.
v.23. All these evil things come from within, and they defile a person.

Luke 8:14
Some don't start out well, and then let the word become choked by cares and riches.
As for what fell among the thorns, these are the ones who hear; but as they go on their way, they are choked by the cares and riches and pleasures of life, and their fruit does not mature.

Acts 13:10
Your life can be full of deceit or walking the simple, straight path.
You son of the devil, you enemy of all righteousness, full of all deceit and villainy, will you not stop making crooked the straight paths of the Lord?

Romans 12:9
Don't let your love be artificial or manipulative.
Let love be genuine; hate what is evil, hold fast to what is good.

1 Corinthians 3:18
Do not deceive yourselves.
Do not deceive yourselves. If you think that you are wise in this age, you should become fools so that you may become wise.

Galatians 6:3
Do not deceive yourselves about who you are.
For if those who are nothing think they are something, they deceive themselves.

1 Timothy 4:7
Learn God's way.
Have nothing to do with profane myths and old wives' tales. Train yourself in godliness.

1 Timothy 6:17
Put your hope on a solid foundation of God and his way.
As for those who in the present age are rich, command them not to be haughty, or to set their hopes on the uncertainty of riches, but rather on God who richly provides us with everything for our enjoyment.

2 Timothy 3:13
Be real and avoid deceit.
But wicked people and impostors will go from bad to worse, deceiving others and being deceived.

2 Timothy 4:4
Stay focused on what is true and good.
And will turn away from listening to the truth and wander away to myths.

James 1:26
Look at how you talk, and at your heart.
If any think they are religious, and do not bridle their tongues but deceive their hearts, their religion is worthless.

1 John 1:6
If your walk is in the dark, you are not in fellowship with God.
If we say that we have fellowship with him while we are walking in darkness, we lie and do not do what is true.

1 John 1:8
Look inside honestly. Look at your inner life.
If we say that we have no sin, we deceive ourselves, and the truth is not in us.

Virtue: Honesty, hope (in right order and God)

Exodus 18:21
You are invited to be a person of truth a leader with integrity.
You should also look for able men among all the people, men who fear God, are trustworthy, and hate dishonest gain; set such men over them as officers over thousands, hundreds, fifties and tens.

Proverbs 3:9
Honor the Lord with your wealth.
Honor the LORD with your substance / and with the first fruits of all your produce.

Proverbs 15:16
Keep a right focus.
Better is a little with the fear of the LORD / than great treasure and trouble with it.

Ezekiel 36:14,27
I will put my Spirit in you. Listen to me.
v.14. Therefore you shall no longer devour people and no longer bereave your nation of children, says the LORD GOD.

v.27. *I will put my spirit within you, and make you follow my statutes and be careful to observe my ordinances.*

Luke 16:10
Be faithful in the little things, and you will be faithful in more.
Whoever is faithful in a very little is faithful also in much; and whoever is dishonest in a very little is dishonest also in much.

John 16:13
He will guide you into all truth.
When the Spirit of truth comes, he will guide you into all the truth; for he will not speak on his own, but will speak whatever he hears, and he will declare to you the things that are to come.

Romans 8:5
Those of the Spirit set their minds on the things of the spirit.
For those who live according to the flesh set their minds on the things of the flesh, but those who live according to the Spirit set their minds on the things of the Spirit.

1 Corinthians 5:8
You are what you eat, so eat the unleavened bread of sincerity and truth.
Therefore, let us celebrate the festival, not with the old yeast, the yeast of malice and evil, but with the unleavened bread of sincerity and truth.

2 Corinthians 1:22
You have your first installment. Invest it wisely.
By putting his seal on us and giving us his Spirit in our hearts as a first installment.

2 Corinthians 3:3
You are a letter written by God for others.
And you show that you are a letter of Christ, prepared by us, written not with ink but with the Spirit of the living God, not on tablets of stone but on tablets of human hearts.

2 Corinthians 5:5
You have a guarantee upon which you can put your trust.
He who has prepared us for this very thing is God, who has given us the Spirit as a guarantee.

Ephesians 6:14
Gird your waist with truth.
Stand therefore, and fasten the belt of truth around your waist, and put on the breastplate of righteousness.

Point Four: Tragic Romantic

Passion: Envy, dissatisfaction, melancholy

Exodus 6:9
The Israelites did not listen because of their depression.
Moses told this to the Israelites; but they would not listen to Moses, because of their broken spirit and their cruel slavery.

Deuteronomy 28:47
You did not serve the Lord with joy.
Because you did not serve the LORD your God joyfully and with gladness of heart for the abundance of everything.

Joshua 9:18
They were dissatisfied and grumbled against their leaders.
Then all the congregation murmured against the leaders.

Proverbs 6:34
Jealousy can enrage and destroy you.
For jealousy arouses a husband's fury, / and he shows no restraint when he takes revenge.

Proverbs 25:20
Continuing in sorrow can wreck your heart.
Like vinegar on a wound / is one who sings songs to a heavy heart. / Like a moth in clothing or a worm in wood, / sorrow gnaws at the human heart.

Ecclesiastes 1:8
Do not live only looking at things with dissatisfaction.
All things are wearisome; / more than one can express; / the eye is not satisfied with seeing, / or the ear filled with hearing.

Song of Songs 8:6
Jealousy is not what you are here for.
Set me as a seal upon your heart, / as a seal upon your arm; / for love is strong as death, / passion fierce as the grave. / Its flashes are flashes of fire, / a raging flame.

Matthew 20:11
Don't live with a heart full of grumbling.
And when they received it, they grumbled against the landowner.

Mark 7:20–23
How you act shows your true heart, the real you.
v.20. It is what comes out of a person that defiles.
v.21. For it is from within, from the human heart, that evil intentions come: fornication, theft, murder.
v.22. Adultery, avarice, wickedness, deceit, licentiousness, envy, slander, pride, folly.
v.23. All these evil things come from within, and they defile a person.

Mark 7:22
Look at your heart, and what you embrace.
Adultery, avarice, wickedness, deceit, licentiousness, envy, slander, pride, folly.

Luke 15:2
Don't set yourself above others.
And the Pharisees and the scribes were grumbling and saying, "This fellow welcomes sinners and eats with them."

Luke 19:7
Don't be one who lives to grumble, judge, or criticize.
All who saw it began to grumble and said, "He has gone to be the guest of one who is a sinner."

Romans 13:13
Do not live with hearts full of friction and jealousy.
Let us live honorably as in the day, not in reveling and drunkenness, not in debauchery and licentiousness, not in quarreling and jealousy.

1 Corinthians 3:3
How you act shows where your heart is.
You are still of the flesh. For as long as there is jealousy and quarreling among you, are you not of the flesh, and behaving according to human inclinations?

1 Corinthians 13:4
Love is not jealous.
Love is patient; love is kind; love is not envious or boastful or arrogant.

2 Corinthians 4:7
You have a very special treasure in a very fragile vessel. Handle it with care.
But we have this treasure in clay jars, so that it may be made clear that this extraordinary power belongs to God and does not come from us.

2 Corinthians 12:20
Live harmoniously without strife and jealousy.
For I fear that when I come, I may find you not as I wish, and that you may find me not as you wish; I fear that there may perhaps be quarreling, jealousy, anger, selfishness, slander, gossip, conceit, and disorder.

Galatians 5:20–21
If you are of God, you will let go of the attitudes not of God.
v.20. Idolatry, sorcery, enmities, strife, jealousy, anger, quarrels, dissensions, factions.
v.21. Envy, drunkenness, carousing, and things like these. I am warning you, as I warned you before: those who do such things will not inherit the kingdom of God.

Galatians 5:26
Do not envy one another.
Let us not become conceited, competing against one another, envying one another.

Philippians 2:14
Do all things without grumbling.
Do all things without murmuring and arguing.

James 3:14,16
Look at your envy and selfish ambition.
v.14. But if you have bitter envy and selfish ambition in your hearts, do not be boastful and false to the truth.
v.16. For where there is envy and selfish ambition, there will also be disorder and wickedness of every kind.

James 5:9
Do not complain against one another.
Beloved, do not grumble against one another, so that you may not be judged. See, the Judge is standing at the doors!

1 Peter 2:1
Put aside all envy.
Rid yourselves, therefore, of all malice, and all guile, insincerity, envy, and all slander.

Virtue: One's original source, harmony and balance

2 Samuel 23:5
You are invited to have a "house" (yourself) full of everything you need.
Is not my house like this with God? / For he has made with me an everlasting covenant, / ordered in all things and secure. / Will he not cause to prosper / all my help and my desire?

Psalm 20:4
The Lord will give you everything you desire.
May he grant you your heart's desire, / and fulfill all your plans.

Psalm 37:4
The Lord will give you everything you desire.
Take delight in the LORD, / and he will give you the desires of your heart.

Psalm 73:25
You are very loved. Receive this love.
Whom have I in heaven but you? / And there is nothing on earth / that I desire other than you.

Psalm 84:2
Let yourself receive joy to satisfy your inner hunger.
My soul longs, indeed it faints / for the courts of the LORD; / my heart and my flesh sing for joy / to the living God.

Psalms 145:19
God is waiting to nurture you. Let him.
He fulfills the desire of all who fear him; / he also hears their cry, and saves them.

Point Five: The Observer

Passion: Avarice, greed, stinginess

Proverbs 1:4
Let your heart be simple, and then you will know wisdom.
To teach shrewdness to the simple, / knowledge and prudence to the young.

Proverbs 2:4
Let your search be for wisdom, carefully, as for hidden treasure.
If you seek it like silver, / and search for it as for hidden treasures.

Proverbs 3:7
The fool is wise in his own eyes.
Do not be wise in your own eyes; fear the LORD, and turn away from evil.

Proverbs 26:12
If you say you are wise, you are a fool.
Do you see persons wise in their own eyes? / There is more hope for fools than for them.

Proverbs 28:11
It is easy to be fooled as to who we really are.
The rich is wise in self-esteem, / but an intelligent poor person sees through the pose.

Ecclesiastes 1:17
Chasing after wisdom is like chasing the wind.
And I applied my mind to know wisdom and to know madness and folly. I perceived that this also is but a chasing after wind.

Isaiah 5:21
Be careful, if you think you are wise.
Ah, you who are wise in your own eyes, / and shrewd in your own sight!

Isaiah 44:25
The Lord will lead you to true knowledge.
Who frustrates the omens of liars, / and makes fools of diviners; / who turns back the wise, / and makes their knowledge foolish.

Jeremiah 8:8–9
The wise are put to shame.
v.8. How can you say, "We are wise, / and the law of the LORD is with us," / when, in fact, the false pen of the scribes / has made it into a lie?
v.9. The wise shall be put to shame, / they shall be dismayed and taken; / since they have rejected the word of the LORD, / what wisdom is in them?

Jeremiah 9:23
The fool is wise in his own eyes.
Thus says the LORD: Do not let the wise boast in their wisdom, do not let the mighty boast in their might, do not let the wealthy boast in their wealth.

Habakkuk 2:5
They protect themselves by storing up things to protect themselves.
Moreover, wealth is treacherous; / the arrogant do not endure. / They open their throats wide as Sheol; / like Death they never have enough. / They gather all nations for themselves, / and collect all peoples as their own.

Romans 12:16
The fool is wise in his own eyes.
Live in harmony with one another; do not be haughty, but associate with the lowly; do not claim to be wiser than you are.

1 Corinthians 2:6
There is a wisdom to which you are called.
Yet among the mature we do speak wisdom, though it is not a wisdom of this age or of the rulers of this age, who are doomed to perish.

1 Corinthians 3:19
The wisdom of this world is foolishness to God.
For the wisdom of this world is foolishness with God. For it is written, / "He catches the wise in their craftiness."

2 Timothy 3:7
The fool is always learning but never coming to know the truth.
Who are always being instructed and can never arrive at a knowledge of the truth.

2 Timothy 4:3
Let your lust for learning be for solid teachings.
For the time is coming when people will not put up with sound doctrine, but having itching ears, they will accumulate for themselves teachers to suit their own desires.

James 1:5
If you lack wisdom, ask God for it.
If any of you is lacking in wisdom, ask God, who gives to all generously and ungrudgingly, and it will be given you.

Virtue: Wisdom, detachment

1 Chronicles 22:12
May the Lord give you prudence.
Only, may the LORD grant you discretion and understanding, so that when he gives you charge over Israel you may keep the law of the LORD your God.

Job 28:28
The fear of the Lord is wisdom.
And he said to humankind, / "Truly, the fear of the Lord, that is wisdom; / and to depart from evil is understanding."

Job 32:7
A day at a time, much wisdom can be learned.
I said, "Let days speak, / and many years teach wisdom."

Psalm 9:10
The fear of the Lord is wisdom.
And those who know your name put their trust in you, / for you, O LORD, have not forsaken those who seek you.

Psalm 111:10
The fear of the Lord is wisdom.
The fear of the LORD is the beginning of wisdom; / all those who practice it have a good understanding. / His praise endures forever.

Proverbs 1:7
The fear of the Lord is wisdom.
The fear of the LORD is the beginning of knowledge; / fools despise wisdom and instruction.

Proverbs 4:5–7
Get wisdom.
v.5. Get wisdom; get insight: do not forget, nor turn away / from the words of my mouth.
v.6. Do not forsake her, and she will keep you; / love her, and she will guard you.
v.7. The beginning of wisdom is this: Get wisdom, / and whatever else you get, get insight.

Ecclesiastes 1:18
You will experience grief as you grow in wisdom.
For in much wisdom is much vexation, / and those who increase knowledge increase sorrow.

Ecclesiastes 2:13
Wisdom exceeds folly as light exceeds darkness.
Then I saw that wisdom excels folly as light excels darkness.

Isaiah 11:2
You can receive the spirit of wisdom and understanding.
The spirit of the LORD shall rest on him, / the spirit of wisdom and understanding, / the spirit of counsel and might, / the spirit of knowledge and the fear of the Lord.

Daniel 2:21
God gives wisdom to the wise.
He changes times and seasons, / deposes kings and sets up kings; / he gives wisdom to the wise / and knowledge to those who have understanding.

Galatians 6:6
Let him who is taught share with him who teaches.
Those who are taught the word must share in all good things with their teacher.

Ephesians 1:8,9
God's wisdom and insight.
That he lavished on us. With all wisdom and insight he has made known to us the mystery of his will.

Ephesians 1:17
God will give you the Spirit of wisdom and revelation.
I pray that the God of our Lord Jesus Christ, the Father of glory, may give you a spirit of wisdom and revelation as you come to know him.

Colossians 2:3
Worthwhile treasure have to be dug for deeply within yourself, and your God.
In whom are hidden all the treasures of wisdom and knowledge.

Hebrews 5:12
You ought by now to be teachers.
For though by this time you ought to be teachers, you need someone to teach you again the basic elements of the oracles of God. You need milk, not solid food.

Point Six: The Devil's Advocate

Passion: Fear, doubt, cowardice

1 Kings 2:6
Act according to your wisdom.
Act therefore according to your wisdom, but do not let his gray head go down to Sheol in peace.

Job 8:14
His trust is fragile as a spider's web.
Their confidence is gossamer, / a spider's house their trust.

Job 38:36
Do you know who has put the wisdom in your mind?
Who has put wisdom in the inward parts, / or given understanding to the mind?

Psalm 19:7
Prudence is given to the simple.
The law of the LORD is perfect, / reviving the soul; / the decrees of the LORD are sure, / making wise the simple.

Proverbs 25:19
Trust in a faithless person like a bad tooth.
Like a bad tooth or a lame foot / is trust in a faithless person in time of trouble.

Isaiah 42:17
Look at the things you need in order to feel secure.
They shall be turned back and utterly put to shame— / those who trust in carved images, / who say to cast images, / "You are our gods."

Jeremiah 48:7
You are foolish. You will only find insecurity if you seek security in a stronghold or in your treasures.
Surely, because you trusted in your strongholds and your treasures, / you also shall be taken.

Matthew 6:25–27
You are invited to let go of worry.
v.25. Therefore I tell you, do not worry about your life, what you will eat or what you will drink, or about your body, what you will wear. Is not life more than food, and the body more than clothing?
v.26. Look at the birds of the air; they neither sow nor reap nor gather into barns, and yet your heavenly Father feeds them. Are you not of more value than they?
v.27. And can any of you by worrying add a single hour to your span of life?

Matthew 6:32–34
You are invited to look to your God, and let go of anxiety, worry, and fear.
v.32. For it is the Gentiles who strive for all these things; and indeed your heavenly Father knows that you need all these things.
v.33. But strive first for the kingdom of God and his righteousness, and all these things will be given to you as well.
v.34. So do not worry about tomorrow, for tomorrow will bring worries of its own. Today's trouble is enough for today.

Matthew 8:26
Why are you afraid? Your faith is so little.
And he said to them, "Why are you afraid, you of little faith?" Then he got up and rebuked the winds and the sea; and there was a dead calm.

Matthew 13:11–21
You will be given knowledge of many things if you stop seeking it so desperately.
v.11. He answered, "To you it has been given to know the secrets of the kingdom of heaven, but to them it has not been given."
v.13. The reason I speak to them in parables is that "seeing they do not perceive, and hearing they do not listen, nor do they understand."
v.14. With them indeed is fulfilled the prophecy of Isaiah that says: / "You

will indeed listen, but never understand, / and you will indeed look, but never perceive."

v.15. *For this people's heart has grown dull, / and their ears are hard of hearing, / and they have shut their eyes; / so that they might not look with their eyes, / and listen with their ears, / and understand with their heart and turn— / and I would heal them.*

v.16. *But blessed are your eyes, for they see, and your ears, for they hear.*

v.17. *Truly I tell you, many prophets and righteous people longed to see what you see, but did not see it, and to hear what you hear, but did not hear it.*

v.18. *Hear then the parable of the sower.*

v.19. *When anyone hears the word of the kingdom and does not understand it, the evil one comes and snatches away what is sown in the heart; this is what was sown on the path.*

v.20. *As for what was sown on rocky ground, this is the one who hears the word and immediately receives it with joy.*

v.21. *Yet such a person has no root, but endures only for a while, and when trouble or persecution arises on account of the word, that person immediately falls away.*

Mark 4:19
Anxiety can choke what is trying to grow in you.
But the cares of the world, and the lure of wealth, and the desire for other things come in and choke the word, and it yields nothing.

Mark 7:20–23
How you act shows your true heart, the real you.
v.20. *It is what comes out of a person that defiles.*

v.21. *For it is from within, from the human heart, that evil intentions come: fornication, theft, murder.*

v.22. *Adultery, avarice, wickedness, deceit, licentiousness, envy, slander, pride, folly.*

v.23. *All these evil things come from within, and they defile a person.*

Mark 9:24
I want to believe, help my unbelief!
Immediately the father of the child cried out, "I believe; help my unbelief!"

Luke 12:11–29

Don't be worried or anxious for anything, for you will have your needs cared for.

v.11. When they bring you before the synagogues, the rulers, and the authorities, do not worry about how you are to defend yourselves or what you are to say.

v.12. For the Holy Spirit will teach you at that very hour what you ought to say.

v.15. And he said to them, "Take care! Be on your guard against all kinds of greed; for one's life does not consist in the abundance of possessions."

v.22. He said to his disciples, "Therefore I tell you, do not worry about your life, what you will eat, or about your body, what you will wear."

v.23. For life is more than food, and the body more than clothing.

v.25. And can any of you by worrying add a single hour to your span of life?

v.26. If then you are not able to do so small a thing as that, why do you worry about the rest?

Luke 21:34

Don't be worried or anxious for anything, your food, what you will do or say.

Be on guard so that your hearts are not weighed down with dissipation and drunkenness and the worries of this life, and that day catch you unexpectedly.

Romans 10:16

The branches were broken off through their unbelief.

But not all have obeyed the good news; for Isaiah says, "Lord, who has believed our message?"

1 Corinthians 7:32

You are invited to be free of your fear.

I want you to be free from anxieties. The unmarried man is anxious about the affairs of the Lord, how to please the Lord.

1 Peter 5:7

You are invited to let go of your fear and anxiety.

Cast all your anxiety on him, because he cares for you.

Revelation 21:8
Living life in fear and cowardice is not worth it.
But as for the cowardly, the faithless…idolaters, and all liars, their place will be in the lake that burns with fire and sulfur, which is the second death.

Virtue: Faith, trust, courage

Deuteronomy 33:12
Your life can be one full of real safety.
Of Benjamin he said: / The beloved of the LORD rests in safety— / the High God surrounds him all day long— / the beloved rests between his shoulders.

2 Kings 18:19
Where does your confidence come from?
On what do you base this confidence of yours?

2 Chronicles 20:20
Have trust, hope, confidence in God at all times.
Listen to me, O Judah and inhabitants of Jerusalem! Believe in the LORD your God and you will be established; believe his prophets.

Psalm 19:7
Prudence is given to the simple.
The law of the Lord is perfect, / reviving the soul; the decrees of the LORD are sure, / making wise the simple.

Psalm 25:2
You will be safe if you trust in God.
O my God, in you I trust; / do not let me be put to shame; / do not let my enemies exult over me.

Psalm 31:6
Put your trust in only one God.
You hate those who pay regard to worthless idols, / but I trust in the LORD.

Psalm 31:14
Have trust, hope, confidence in God at all times
But I trust in you, O LORD; / I say, "You are my God."

Psalm 40:4
You can know happiness and perfect peace if you trust.
*Happy are those who make / the L*ORD *their trust, / who do not turn to the proud, / to those who go astray after false gods.*

Psalm 42:5,11
Trust in God can wipe away the worst anxiety and turmoil.
v.5. Why are you cast down, O my soul, / and why are you disquieted within me? / Hope in God; for I shall again praise him, / my help and my God.
v.11. Why are you cast down, O my soul, / and why are you disquieted within me? / Hope in God; for I shall again praise him, / my help and my God.

Psalm 43:5
Have trust and your anxiety and turmoil will leave you.
Why are you cast down, O my soul, / and why are you disquieted within me? / Hope in God; for I shall again praise him, / my help and my God.

Psalm 55:23
Have trust, hope, confidence in God no matter how hard your life becomes.
But you, O God, will cast them down / into the lowest pit; / the bloodthirsty and treacherous / shall not live out half their days. / But I will trust in you.

Psalm 84:12
You will have happiness if you can trust.
*O L*ORD *of hosts, / happy is everyone who trusts in you.*

Isaiah 50:10
Trust and you will have hope no matter what troubles come your way.
*Who among you fears the L*ORD */ and obeys the voice of his servant, / who walks in darkness / and has no light, / yet trusts in the name of the L*ORD */ and relies upon his God?*

Matthew 21:22
Prayer will be answered if you ask with faith.
Whatever you ask for in prayer with faith, you will receive.

Mark 11:22
Trust in God at all times.
Jesus answered them, "Have faith in God."

Mark 11:24
Your prayer will be answered if you ask with belief.
So I tell you, whatever you ask for in prayer, believe that you have received it, and it will be yours.

John 7:38
You will be living for others if you accept to believe.
And let the one who believes in me drink. As the scripture has said, "Out of the believer's heart shall flow rivers of living water."

1 Corinthians 12:9
Faith is a spiritual gift.
To another faith by the same Spirit, to another gifts of healing by the one Spirit.

2 Corinthians 1:22
You have been given the Spirit of God within you as a pledge of security.
By putting his seal on us and giving us his Spirit in our hearts as a first installment.

1 Thessalonians 5:8
Clothe yourself with faith, hope, and love.
But since we belong to the day, let us be sober, and put on the breastplate of faith and love, and for a helmet the hope of salvation.

1 Timothy 1:5
Let your goal be to have a sincere faith.
But the aim of such instruction is love that comes from a pure heart, a good conscience, and sincere faith.

1 Timothy 6:12
Fight the good fight of faith.
Fight the good fight of the faith; take hold of the eternal life, to which you were called and for which you made the good confession in the presence of many witnesses.

Hebrews 11:4–40
You are called to act out of your faith.
v.4. By faith Abel offered to God a more acceptable sacrifice than Cain's. Through this he received approval as righteous, God himself giving approval to his gifts; he died, but through his faith he still speaks.
v.6. And without faith it is impossible to please God, for whoever would approach him must believe that he exists and that he rewards those who seek him.
v.7. By faith Noah, warned by God about events as yet unseen, respected the warning and built an ark to save his household; by this he condemned the world and became an heir to the righteousness that is in accordance with faith.
v.8. By faith Abraham obeyed when he was called to set out for a place that he was to receive as an inheritance; and he set out, not knowing where he was going.
v.11. By faith he received power of procreation, even though he was too old—and Sarah herself was barren—because he considered him faithful who had promised.
v.12. Therefore from one person, and this one as good as dead, descendants were born, "as many as the stars of heaven and as the innumerable grains of sand by the seashore."
v.16. But as it is, they desire a better country, that is, a heavenly one. Therefore God is not ashamed to be called their God; indeed, he has prepared a city for them.
v.17. By faith Abraham, when put to the test, offered up Isaac. He who had received the promises was ready to offer up his only son.
v.23. By faith Moses was hidden by his parents for three months after his birth, because they saw that the child was beautiful; and they were not afraid of the king's edict.
v.25. Choosing rather to share ill-treatment with the people of God than to enjoy the fleeting pleasures of sin.
v.26. He considered abuse suffered for the Christ to be greater wealth than the treasures of Egypt, for he was looking ahead to the reward.

v.27. *By faith he left Egypt, unafraid of the king's anger; for he persevered as though he saw him who is invisible.*

v.30. *By faith the walls of Jericho fell after they had been encircled for seven days.*

v.33. *Who through faith conquered kingdoms, administered justice, obtained promises, shut the mouths of lions.*

v.34. *Quenched raging fire, escaped the edge of the sword, won strength out of weakness, became mighty in war, put foreign armies to flight.*

James 1:6

Ask in faith, not doubting.

But ask in faith, never doubting, for the one who doubts is like a wave of the sea, driven and tossed by the wind.

1 Peter 1:21

Have trust, hope, confidence in God at all times.

Through him you have come to trust in God, who raised him from the dead and gave him glory, so that your faith and hope are set on God.

Point Seven: The Planner

Passion: Gluttony, mental and physical

Numbers 21:4

Don't be so hasty and impatient.

From Mount Hor they set out by the way to the Red Sea, to go around the land of Edom; but the people became impatient on the way.

Joshua 24:23

Put away your foreign gods.

He said, "Then put away the foreign gods that are among you, and incline your hearts to the LORD, the God of Israel."

Ecclesiastes 7:3

Don't be afraid to allow sorrow to come inside you.

Sorrow is better than laughter, / for by sadness of countenance the heart is made glad.

Ecclesiastes 7:9
Don't be so hasty to lash out at others.
Do not be quick to anger, / for anger lodges in the bosom of fools.

Psalm 52:3
Look at what you love, what draws your attention.
You love evil more than good, / and lying more than speaking the truth.

Proverbs 21:2
Everyone's way is right in his own eyes.
All deeds are right in the sight of the doer, / but the LORD weighs the heart.

Isaiah 30:1
Woe to those who carry out a plan, if not mine.
Oh, rebellious children, says the LORD, / who carry out a plan, but not mine; / who make an alliance, but against my will, / adding sin to sin.

Isaiah 55:8
My ways are not your ways.
For my thoughts are not your thoughts, / nor are your ways my ways, says the LORD.

Jeremiah 9:3
Don't use your tongue to hurt others.
They bend their tongues like bows; / they have grown strong in the land for falsehood, and not for truth; / for they proceed from evil to evil, / and they do not know me, says the LORD.

Matthew 15:9
Be careful of the teachings you receive.
In vain do they worship me, / teaching human precepts as doctrines.

Mark 7:7
Be careful of the teachings you receive.
In vain do they worship me, / teaching human precepts as doctrines.

Mark 7:20–23
How you act shows your true heart, the real you.
v.20. It is what comes out of a person that defiles.

v.21. *For it is from within, from the human heart, that evil intentions come: fornication, theft, murder.*
v.22. *Adultery, avarice, wickedness, deceit, licentiousness, envy, slander, pride, folly.*
v.23. *All these evil things come from within, and they defile a person.*

Ephesians 4:14
Do not be blown from side to side by every new wind of teaching.
We must no longer be children, tossed to and fro and blown about by every wind of doctrine, by people's trickery, by their craftiness in deceitful scheming.

2 Timothy 3:4
Don't live so recklessly, loving pleasure more than your God.
Treacherous, reckless, swollen with conceit, lovers of pleasure rather than lovers of God.

2 Timothy 3:7
Look for deep inner knowledge, not only always seeking new learning.
Who are always being instructed and can never arrive at a knowledge of the truth.

2 Timothy 4:3
Look for teachers of the truth, not only teachers to satisfy your own lusts.
For the time is coming when people will not put up with sound doctrine, but having itching ears, they will accumulate for themselves teachers to suit their own desires.

Virtue: Sobriety, holy work

2 Samuel 6:14,16
Let your joy be a praise of the Lord.
*David danced before the L*ORD *with all his might; David was girded with a linen ephod.*

1 Chronicles 15:29
Praise his name with your delight and your dancing.
As the ark of the covenant of the LORD *came to the city of David, Michal daughter of Saul looked out of the window, and saw King David leaping and dancing; and she despised him in her heart.*

Psalm 45:7
You will be blessed with great happiness and joy.
You love righteousness and hate wickedness. / Therefore God, your God, has anointed you / with the oil of gladness beyond your companions.

Proverbs 16:1–9
It is good to plan, but let the Lord also show you the way.
The plans of the mind belong to mortals, / but the answer of the tongue is from the LORD.

Proverbs 16:3,9
Let God help you with your plans.
v.3. Commit your work to the LORD, */ and your plans will be established.*
v.9. The human mind plans the way, but the LORD *directs the steps.*

Proverbs 19:21
It is good to plan, but let the Lord direct your way, as well.
The human mind may devise many plans, / but it is the purpose of the LORD *that will be established.*

Ecclesiastes 3:4
There is a time to laugh and dance.
A time to weep, and a time to laugh; / a time to mourn, and a time to dance.

Romans 12:12
Live with a happy heart, patient with suffering, and very prayerfully.
Rejoice in hope, be patient in suffering, persevere in prayer.

1 Thessalonians 5:16
Live with a happy heart.
Rejoice always.

Hebrews 1:9
You have been given the gift of your happiness and joy.
You have loved righteousness and hated wickedness; / therefore God, your God, has anointed you / with the oil of gladness beyond your companions.

Point Eight: The Boss

Passion: Lust

Numbers 21:4
Do not be hasty or reckless.
From Mount Hor they set out by the way to the Red Sea, to go around the land of Edom; but the people became impatient on the way.

Joshua 22:16,18
Are you turning away from the Lord?
v.16. Thus says the whole congregation of the LORD, "What is this treachery that you have committed against the God of Israel in turning away today from following the LORD, by building yourselves an altar today in rebellion against the LORD?"
v.18. That you must turn away today from following the LORD! If you rebel against the LORD today, he will be angry with the whole congregation of Israel tomorrow.

Joshua 24:23
Put away your foreign gods.
He said, "Then put away the foreign gods that are among you, and incline your hearts to the LORD, the God of Israel."

2 Samuel 12:6
He must pay four times over because he had no pity.
He shall restore the lamb fourfold, because he did this thing, and because he had no pity.

1 Kings 18:18
You have broken the Lord's command.
He answered, "I have not troubled Israel; but you have, and your father's house, because you have forsaken the commandments of the LORD and followed the Baals."

2 Chronicles 7:19
Open up to see your false gods.
But if you turn aside and forsake my statutes and my commandments that I have set before you, and go and serve other gods and worship them.

Job 31:29
Are you happy when bad things happen to people who hurt you?
If I have rejoiced at the ruin of those who hated me, / or exulted when evil overtook them.

Psalm 17:10
Don't judge harshly. Love humbly.
They close their hearts to pity; / with their mouths they speak arrogantly.

Psalm 37:5
Commit your way to the Lord.
Commit your way to the LORD; / trust in him, and he will act.

Psalm 50:17
Do you hate discipline and ignore God?
For you hate discipline, / and you cast my words behind you.

Proverbs 1:25,30
You don't listen to my message or correction.
And because you have ignored all my counsel / and would have none of my reproof.

Proverbs 13:18
Open up to listening to encouragement from others.
Poverty and disgrace are for the one who ignores instruction, / but one who heeds reproof is honored.

Proverbs 22:15
Open up to discipline so that you may be mature.
Folly is bound up in the heart of a boy, / but the rod of discipline drives it far away.

Ecclesiastes 2:1,10
Pleasure and self are empty, and have no lasting value.
v.1. I said to myself, "Come now, I will make a test of pleasure; enjoy your-self." But again, this also was vanity.
v.10. Whatever my eyes desired I did not keep from them; I kept my heart from no pleasure, for my heart found pleasure in all my toil, and this was my reward for all my toil.

Ecclesiastes 2:17
They found that chasing pleasure was like chasing the wind.
So I hated life, because what is done under the sun was grievous to me; for all is vanity and a chasing after wind.

Isaiah 57:4,5
You are full of evil if you live for your lust.
v.4. Are you not children of transgression.
v.5. You that burn with lust among the oaks, / under every green tree; / you that slaughter your children in the valleys, / under the clefts of the rocks?

Jeremiah 2:13
Put away your foreign gods.
For my people have committed two evils: / they have forsaken me, / the fountain of living water, / and dug out cisterns for themselves, / cracked cisterns that can hold no water.

Jeremiah 2:24
You are like a wild ass in heat.
A wild ass at home in the wilderness, / in her heat sniffing the wind! / Who can restrain her lust? / None who seek her need weary themselves; / in her month they will find her.

Jeremiah 10:23
You can't control everything in your life.
I know, O LORD, that the way of human beings is not in their control, / that mortals as they walk cannot direct their steps.

Jeremiah 18:15
Look at where you are really walking.
But my people have forgotten me, / they burn offerings to a delusion; / they have stumbled in their ways, / in the ancient roads, / and have gone into bypaths, / not the highway.

Hosea 14:4
I will heal their backsliding.
I will heal their disloyalty; / I will love them freely, / for my anger has turned from them.

Hosea 14:9
My ways are right, but they are not your ways.
Those who are wise understand these things; / those who are discerning know them. / For the ways of the LORD are right, / and the upright walk in them, / but transgressors stumble in them.

Habakkuk 3:12
You are a fool if you lash out at others and trample them.
In fury you trod the earth, / in anger you trampled nations.

Matthew 5:28
If you look lustfully, you have committed adultery.
But I say to you that everyone who looks at a woman with lust has already committed adultery with her in his heart.

Mark 7:20–23
How you act shows your true heart, the real you.
v.20. It is what comes out of a person that defiles.
v.21. For it is from within, from the human heart, that evil intentions come: fornication, theft, murder.
v.22. Adultery, avarice, wickedness, deceit, licentiousness, envy, slander, pride, folly.
v.23. All these evil things come from within, and they defile a person.

Luke 21:34
Be careful that you don't wreck your life with drunkenness and anxiety.
Be on guard so that your hearts are not weighed down with dissipation and drunkenness and the worries of this life, and that day catch you unexpectedly.

Romans 1:28–32
Look at your behavior and see where your heart is.
v.28. And since they did not see fit to acknowledge God, God gave them up to a debased mind and to things that should not be done.
v.29. They were filled with every kind of wickedness, evil, covetousness, malice. Full of envy, murder, strife, deceit, craftiness, they are gossips.
v.30. Slanderers, God-haters, insolent, haughty, boastful, inventors of evil, rebellious toward parents.
v.32. They know God's decree, that those who practice such things deserve to die—yet they not only do them but even applaud others who practice them.

Galatians 1:6
Don't turn away from his ways.
I am astonished that you are so quickly deserting the one who called you in the grace of Christ and are turning to a different gospel.

2 Thessalonians 2:12
Don't take pleasure in sin.
So that all who have not believed the truth but took pleasure in unrighteousness will be condemned.

2 Timothy 3:4
Do not choose ways other than God's way.
Treacherous, reckless, swollen with conceit, lovers of pleasure rather than lovers of God.

Hebrews 12:9
Submit to God, the Father of all spirits.
Moreover, we had human parents to discipline us, and we respected them. Should we not be even more willing to be subject to the Father of spirits and live?

James 4:7
Submit to God, the Father of all spirits.
Submit yourselves therefore to God. Resist the devil, and he will flee from you.

1 Peter 2:11
Your lusts are making a way inside you.
Beloved, I urge you as aliens and exiles to abstain from the desires of the flesh that wage war against the soul.

2 Peter 1:4
The world's corruption comes through lust and excesses.
Thus he has given us, through these things, his precious and very great promises, so that through them you may escape from the corruption that is in the world because of lust, and may become participants of the divine nature.

2 Peter 2:10
The proud are not afraid to slander others for their own satisfaction.
Especially those who indulge their flesh in depraved lust, and who despise authority. Bold and willful, they are not afraid to slander the glorious ones.

2 Peter 2:18
They are loud, lustful, and lead the weaker ones down the wrong path as well.
For they speak bombastic nonsense, and with licentious desires of the flesh they entice people who have just escaped from those who live in error.

Revelations 3:19
Those whom I love I reprove and instruct.
I reprove and discipline those whom I love. Be earnest, therefore, and repent.

Virtue: Innocence, compassion

Exodus 18:21
The man of truth shall be the leader.
You should also look for able men among all the people, men who fear God, are trustworthy, and hate dishonest gain; set such men over them as officers over thousands, hundreds, fifties and tens.

1 Kings 21:7
You will eat rejoicing in the ways of the Lord.
His wife Jezebel said to him, "Do you now govern Israel? Get up, eat some food, and be cheerful; I will give you the vineyard of Naboth the Jezreelite."

Psalm 28:2
Humbly lift up your heart, your hands, holy hands to heaven.
Hear the voice of my supplication, / as I cry to you for help, / as I lift up my hands / toward your most holy sanctuary.

Psalm 37:4
He will give you the desires of your heart.
Take delight in the LORD, / and he will give you the desires of your heart.

Psalm 42:2
Let yourself experience a thirst for God and his way.
My soul thirsts for God, / for the living God. / When shall I come and behold the face of God?

Psalm 63:1
Let yourself hunger and thirst for God and his way.
O God, you are my God, I seek you, / my soul thirsts for you; / my flesh faints for you, / as in a dry and weary land where there is no water.

Psalm 63:4
Live to lift holy hands in praise to God.
So I will bless you as long as I live; / I will lift up my hands and call on your name.

Psalm 119:20,40,48
Let yourself experience longing for his commandments and teachings.
v.20. My soul is consumed with longing / for your ordinances at all times.
v.40. See, I have longed for your precepts; / in your righteousness give me life.
v.48. I revere your commandments, which I love, / and I will meditate on your statutes.

Matthew 5:7
Let your way be merciful and kind.
Blessed are the merciful, for they will receive mercy.

Matthew 9:13
Give up your arrogance, and embrace a way of mercy.
Go and learn what this means, "I desire mercy, not sacrifice." For I have come to call not the righteous but sinners.

Matthew 12:7
Don't judge others so harshly.
But if you had known what this means, "I desire mercy and not sacrifice," you would not have condemned the guiltless.

Matthew 18:33
Show mercy to others.
Should you not have had mercy on your fellow slave, as I had mercy on you?

Mark 7:20–23
How you act shows your true heart, the real you.
v.20. It is what comes out of a person that defiles.
v.21. For it is from within, from the human heart, that evil intentions come: fornication, theft, murder.
v.22. Adultery, avarice, wickedness, deceit, licentiousness, envy, slander, pride, folly.
v.23. All these evil things come from within, and they defile a person.

Romans 13:8–10
Live with love for your neighbor, and you will be living well.
v.8. Owe no one anything, except to love one another; for the one who loves another has fulfilled the law.
v.9. The commandments, "You shall not commit adultery; You shall not murder; You shall not steal; You shall not covet"; and any other commandment, are summed up in this word, "Love your neighbor as yourself."
v.10. Love does no wrong to a neighbor; therefore, love is the fulfilling of the law.

Galatians 5:22
Your life is good and true when you live these fruits.
By contrast, the fruit of the Spirit is love, joy, peace, patience, kindness, generosity, faithfulness.

Ephesians 4:32
Be kindhearted, tender, and forgiving with others.
And be kind to one another, tenderhearted, forgiving one another, as God in Christ has forgiven you.

Colossians 3:12
Clothe yourselves with compassion.
As God's chosen ones, holy and beloved, clothe yourselves with compassion, kindness, humility, meekness, and patience.

1 Timothy 2:8
Let your life be free of anger and argument.
I desire, then, that in every place the men should pray, lifting up holy hands without anger or argument.

Hebrews 11:25
Move beyond pleasure to embrace the sufferings of others with them.
Choosing rather to share ill-treatment with the people of God than to enjoy the fleeting pleasures of sin.

Point Nine: The Peacemaker

Passion: Sloth (self-forgetting)

Exodus 32:9
They just won't submit or listen.
The LORD said to Moses, "I have seen this people, how stiff-necked they are."

Exodus 33:3,5
Don't be so stiff-necked.
v.3. Go up to a land flowing with milk and honey; but I will not go up among you, or I would consume you on the way, for you are a stiff-necked people.
v.5. For the LORD had said to Moses, "Say to the Israelites, 'You are a stiff-necked people; if for a single moment I should go up among you, I would consume you. So now take off your ornaments, and I will decide what to do to you.'"

Numbers 11:4
They were greedy for food.
The rabble among them had a strong craving; and the Israelites also wept again, and said, "If only we had meat to eat!"

Deuteronomy 9:6,13
My people are so stiff-necked.
v.6. Know, then, that the LORD your God is not giving you this good land to occupy because of your righteousness; for you are a stubborn people.
v.13. Furthermore the LORD said to me, "I have seen that this people is indeed a stubborn people."

1 Samuel 6:6
Why don't you listen to God?
Why should you harden your hearts as the Egyptians and Pharaoh hardened their hearts? After he had made fools of them, did they not let the people go, and they departed?

2 Samuel 2:21
Do not be easily swayed, turning from your goal so easily.
Abner said to him, "Turn to your right or to your left, and seize one of the young men, and take his spoil." But Asahel would not turn away from following him.

2 Kings 17:14
They would not listen and believe.
They would not listen but were stubborn, as their ancestors had been, who did not believe in the LORD their God.

Nehemiah 9:17
Don't live taking on slavery in any way.
They refused to obey, and were not mindful of the wonders that you performed among them; but they stiffened their necks and determined to return to their slavery in Egypt.

Nehemiah 9:29
Listen to others when they try to teach you.
And you warned them in order to turn them back to your law. Yet they acted presumptuously and did not obey your commandments, but sinned against your ordinances, by the observance of which a person shall live. They turned a stubborn shoulder and stiffened their neck and would not obey.

Psalm 81:12
Be careful that you do not remain in your stubbornness.
So I gave them over to their stubborn hearts, / to follow their own counsels.

Isaiah 48:4
Don't be so obstinate.
Because I know that you are obstinate, / and your neck is an iron sinew / and your forehead brass.

Isaiah 51:17
You are asleep to what is important. You are dulling your senses. Wake up!
Rouse yourself, rouse yourself! / Stand up, O Jerusalem, / you who have drunk at the hand of the LORD / the cup of his wrath, / who have drunk to the dregs / the bowl of staggering.

Jeremiah 17:23
Open up to the message when it comes.
Yet they did not listen or incline their ear; they stiffened their necks and would not hear or receive instruction.

Luke 9:62
Don't forget your goal. Remain faithful to your path.
Jesus said to him, "No one who puts a hand to the plow and looks back is fit for the kingdom of God."

Romans 13:11
You are asleep to what is important. Wake up!
Besides this, you know what time it is, how it is now the moment for you to wake from sleep. For salvation is nearer to us now than when we became believers.

Romans 14:19
Don't slack off from working for peace and harmony.
Let us then pursue what makes for peace and for mutual upbuilding.

2 Corinthians 5:18–19
Your work is the ministry of reconciliation.
v.18. All this is from God, who reconciled us to himself through Christ, and has given us the ministry of reconciliation.
v.19. That is, in Christ God was reconciling the world to himself, not counting their trespasses against them, and entrusting the message of reconciliation to us.

Philippians 3:19
Your god is your belly.
Their end is destruction; their god is the belly; and their glory is in their shame; their minds are set on earthly things.

1 Thessalonians 4:11
Make it your ambition to lead a quiet life, doing work.
To aspire to live quietly, to mind your own affairs, and to work with your hands, as we directed you.

2 Thessalonians 3:10
If someone refuses to work, he shall not eat.
For even when we were with you, we gave you this command: Anyone unwilling to work should not eat.

James 2:17–26
Unless you show your faith by good works, it is dead.
v.17. So faith by itself, if it has no works, is dead.
v.18. But someone will say, "You have faith and I have works." Show me your faith apart from your works, and I by my works will show you my faith.

v.20. *Do you want to be shown, you senseless person, that faith apart from works is barren?*

James 2:22,26
Faith is made complete by good works.
v.22. You see that faith was active along with his works, and faith was brought to completion by the works.
v.26. For just as the body without the spirit is dead, so faith without works is also dead.

1 Peter 2:25
Remain on your path.
For you were going astray like sheep, but now you have returned to the shepherd and guardian of your souls.

1 Peter 3:11
Seek peace and pursue it.
Let them turn away from evil and do good; / let them seek peace and pursue it.

Revelation 3:15–16
You are lukewarm, neither cold nor hot.
v.15. I know your works; you are neither cold nor hot. I wish that you were either cold or hot.
v.16. So, because you are lukewarm, and neither cold nor hot, I am about to spit you out of my mouth.

Virtue: Right action, peace

Psalm 46:10
Slow down and listen to your God.
Be still, and know that I am God! / I am exalted among the nations, / I am exalted in the earth.

Isaiah 26:3
If you really believe, you have perfect peace.
Those of steadfast mind you keep in peace— / in peace because they trust in you.

Isaiah 48:18
If you had obeyed, your peace would be like a flowing river.
O that you had paid attention to my commandments! / Then your prosperity would have been like a river, / and your success like the waves of the sea.

Matthew 5:33
Complete the work you begin, and fulfill your vows.
Again, you have heard that it was said to those of ancient times, "You shall not swear falsely, but carry out the vows you have made to the Lord."

Matthew 7:24
If you hear God's word, do his work.
Everyone then who hears these words of mine and acts on them will be like a wise man who built his house on rock.

Matthew 21:29
It is good to change your way back to God.
He answered, "I will not"; but later he changed his mind and went.

Luke 6:47
If you hear his word, do his work.
I will show you what someone is like who comes to me, hears my words, and acts on them.

John 7:38
From your belief will come living water for others.
And let the one who believes in me drink. As the scripture has said, "Out of the believer's heart shall flow rivers of living water."

John 14:10
You can feel as if God is doing everything for you.
Do you not believe that I am in the Father and the Father is in me? The words that I say to you I do not speak on my own; but the Father who dwells in me does his works.

Romans 14:19
Don't slack off from working for peace and harmony.
Let us then pursue what makes for peace and for mutual upbuilding.

Ephesians 2:10
You are God's workmanship.
For we are what he has made us, created in Christ Jesus for good works, which God prepared beforehand to be our way of life.

Ephesians 2:14
Let yourself enjoy peace from him.
For he is our peace; in his flesh he has made both groups into one and has broken down the dividing wall, that is, the hostility between us.

Philippians 2:13
God is moving in you, to strengthen you in your choices, and to help you to work.
For it is God who is at work in you, enabling you both to will and to work for his good pleasure.

Colossians 4:17
Complete the work you begin and fulfill your vows.
And say to Archippus, "See that you complete the task that you have received in the Lord."

Notes

[1] The following abbreviations are used for the literature cited in this section.

AA:	*Alcoholics Anonymous* (This is also referred to as the "Big Book of A.A." by those in the AA Program.
12/12:	*Twelve Steps and Twelve Traditions*
Bill Sees:	*As Bill Sees It*
AA Comes Age:	*Alcoholics Anonymous Comes of Age*

[2] The Twelve Steps are reprinted with permission of Alcoholics Anonymous World Services, Inc. Permission to reprint and adapt this material does not mean that AA has reviewed or approved the content of this publication, nor that AA agrees with the views expressed herein. AA is a program of recovery from alcoholism *only*—use of the Twelve Steps in connection with programs and activities that are patterned after AA but that address other problems, does not imply otherwise.

Index

A

"Accident"
  Coincidence 6
Action 5
Affirmation 70
Aggressive 30
Ambitious 31
Amends 7
  Amends 7
Angry
  Anger 13
Anonymous
  Anonymous 6
Anxious 25
Approval 28
Arrows 14
Ask 6
Attention 23
Attractive 37

B

Believe 6
Breathe
  Breath 69

C

Centering 133

Characteristics 14
Clean House 8
Companion 70
Conscious Contact 7
Contemplation 134

D

Death 41
Defects
  Defects 6
Director 22
Dissatisfaction 37
Drummer 36

E

Ego 8
Envy 37
Eyes 21

F

Failure 32
Fear
  Fear 6
Feeling
  Feelings 6
Five Steppers 156
Fixations 22

G

Gifts
  Gifts 6
Glasses 8
God 6,7
  God v
God Box 136

H

Hurts 6
H.A.L.T. 129
Harms 6
Higher Power 5
Humility 102

I

Instinct/Subtype 26
Instincts
  Subtypes 9
Inventory 6
Issues 22

J

Jealousy 26
Journaling 123

K

K.I.S.S. 162

L

Lamentation 37
Let 6
Let go
  Let go 6
Let God
  Let God 6
List
  List 7

M

Maintain 7
Masculinity/Femininity 35
Me-First 31
Meditation 132
Melancholy 37
Message 7
Mini-Retreat 138

N

Naranjo 10
Needs 12
New 5
Non-Adaptable 26

O

Obsession 23
One-on-one Instinct/Subtype 26

P

Perceived by Others 24
Perfectionism 23
Personal Behavior 24
Point Eight 30
Point Five 40
Point Four 25
Point Nine 34
Point One 22
Point Seven 25
Point Six 34
Point Three 32
Point Two 27
Powerless 6
  Stuck 6
Pray 6
Prayer 71
Prestige 35
Pride 28
Professionals 129
  Professionals 129

R

Reflective Reading 134
Relationships 6
Remove 6
Resentment 14
Review 6
Right 7

S

Scriptures 71
Security 13
Seductive 28
Self-Deception 32
Serve Others 8
Sex 6
Sides 26
Step Eleven 7
Step Five 6
Step Four 6
Step Nine 7
Step One 6
Step Seven 6
Step Six 6
Step Ten 7
Step Three 6
Step Twelve 7
Step Two 6
Stuck 6
Subtypes
    Instincts 26
Surrender 27
    Surrender 6
Symptoms 130

T

Three levels 7
Traits 22
Treasure 136
Trust God 8
Turn 6
Two Steppers 154

U

Unmanageable 6

V

Vanity 32
Virtue 13

W

Wings 26
Work 6
World 6
Worried 27
Wrongs 7

About the Author

Mary E. Mortz, a Roman Catholic Sister, holds Ph.Ds in Rehabilitation in Special Education and in Religious Studies. She serves as a mentor teacher for the Los Angeles County Office of Education Divisions of Court schools, Alternative Schools, and Special Education.

Mary Mortz is a certified teacher of the Enneagram. For more than fifteen years she has served as spiritual director with special emphasis on prayer, twelve step recovery and the Enneagram. She has published articles on spirituality, spiritual growth, and ministry with the disabled and disability options.

Currently she is do-director of religious formation for her community, the Daughters of Mary and Joseph. She likes to bike, hike, read espionage novels, and write. She is working on an easy to read Scripture series and a book on continuing formation for religious and laity.